RUNNING
WITH
KNIVES

MY GEOMETRIC PATH

HEATHER HAWK

ISBN: 979-8-9882718-1-9 (Paperback)
ISBN: 979-8-9882718-0-2 (Ebook)

Book cover photos: Heather Hawk

Contents

* Vignettes with an asterisk are adapted and expanded upon from my stories in an anthology, "Tales From a Writers' Circle", published May 2023 and/or from my book "Why Be Idle When You Can Run With Knives", published August 2023.

DEDICATION

*In memory of a loyal friend Robert
Collazo Verdecias. D 2020.
Let his words
and thoughts not be forgotten.*

"To my friend I thank you,
for all you have done.
for you were there in the winter
helping me through the snow
showing me the beauty of what I have never known."

A Letter to My Readers

I wish that I had always written and recorded my travels, adventures, and the more interesting highlights of the jobs I have held. Memory fails as does the strong emotions held during the actual time.

Now that I am writing I look back and write about many of the things I have done and accomplished, or things that have happened to me. I am learning a lot about myself. Lessons learned. Things I could have done better.

What kind of person would I be today, had I written day-by-day and learned more about myself at an early age? Emerging patterns would have been seen and would have led to learning and recognizing my skills earlier in life and then building upon those skills. I would not have waited until I was 37 to wake up and acknowledge what I wanted to do or to be in life.

So now, I write every day. Even if I write, "I did nothing today" or "Nothing was accomplished today." This helps me to know where I have been, and what I have accomplished and learned. I highlight important events or things I might want to know more about and remember in the future. This process organizes ideas for where I may go in the future.

These stories are not linear. And why should they be? That has been my life of non-linear, sometimes circuitous, geometric paths. Although I have been known to be spontaneous, I carefully plan and try to have back-up plans as well.

Feel free to jump around the chapters and read out of sequence. The 'Ride of a Life' story may be a bit gruesome for some; but overall, you will find some fun and unusual tales.

I do hope that you enjoy reading my version of my truth.

Read, learn, have fun, and stay sharp. I'd love to know which story you liked best.

www.heatherhawk.net
Heather

P.S. Names have been changed to protect the privacy of friends and family. The stories are from my viewpoint unless stated otherwise.

Preface

Betrayal of Trust

My mother had given me a diary. "Here, this is for you. You can write your thoughts and what you do every day. It has a little locket, so no one can open it. It is your secret."

I was so excited to have something precious to me. I was an avid reader and now I could write too. I began writing as soon as she left the room. I wrote a little something every day, until the betrayal.

After that age of seven, my mother and I were never close, although she wanted to be. My husband relayed to me her lament, that she did not understand her daughter.

"I think our relationship has always been strained. We both wanted to be 'the boss', as we were both headstrong vying to take control of activities. Perhaps it was because of this confrontation. A little act that tore us apart, the dividing line between me and my mother."

"That's mine!" I cried. I had entered my bedroom and found my mother sitting on my bed reading my private diary. My early entrance from school had surprised her. Startled, her eyes opened wide, "Oh, I am sorry. I wanted to see what you wrote."

I grabbed the little cloth book from her and threw it in my garbage can. "So there! No one is supposed to read that! I will never write in it again. And you won't know anything. I hate you!" I cried out with anger and hurt in my voice.

Joseph was sympathetic, "It was not right that your mother betrayed your trust and read your diary. It was your personal story, only to be shared if you chose to."

That little betrayal not only tore our relationship apart, it also repressed my thoughts to put words on paper.

* * *

The first time I can remember being given an essay writing assignment was in third grade. The walls came down-the mind went blank. I did not know a thing about the given subject matter. How could I put anything together? There were no thoughts. Then I recalled a dream that I could write about. The ideas and vision were there; however, the words did not seem to flow. I couldn't make the words appear coherent on paper. I really struggled through that first writing assignment. That struggle continued throughout my school life.

My mother tried another approach to encourage and improve my writing skills. Pen-pals. I would write letters to children in other states, relatives who lived far away and keep in contact with friends we had met in other countries. This letter writing, I felt, was practical, factual and easy. I enjoyed the format tremendously and still pen write letters today.

In high school, another writing assignment was to describe how something worked. What? I was not mechanical and didn't know how anything worked. I thought for hours about a possible object. What simple design would interest me enough that I would want to know the details and could explain a process in simple terms? A ball point pen appeared in front of me. Yes! No one else would write about a simple pen. I researched the topic and wrote an essay about 'Bic' roll ball pens and gravity.

Upon handing me the graded paper the teacher remarked, "That's not what I meant in describing how something works." Obviously he was not impressed and had marked my paper with a red "D".

Did he give an example or a topic when he gave the assignment? No. In those days, teachers were not questioned. Another student wrote about the game of tennis. As I listened to him read his essay, I thought, *Big deal. A sport is not a material thing.* Had I improvised, I could have written details about requirements and skills needed to pass the various levels of proficiency in ice skating. That essay might have received an "A+".

Thus the end of my writing career...until I entered the business world.

When I entered the business world, I learned the formal format for writing business letters. My superiors recognized that I wrote letters that were succinct, clear and to the point. Naturally! The letters made sense. No need for pomp or flowery words. That was real writing. There was something definite to write about.

My father became very sick in 1999 and passed in 2000. Relatives encouraged me to write about his soap opera life. To de-stress from his passing I turned to writing about birds and butterflies for a garden club state magazine. Then as newsletter editor for a plant society. After 2018, I have concentrated more on writing about life.

In my retirement years, for fun and learning, I've transitioned to writing about feelings and accomplishments.

When I first heard about the autobiography/memoir assignment, the walls came down and the mind went blank. What have I ever done that any inner strength was there to guide me? I have long felt to be a pawn in life's game - a re-actor, not a pro-actor. I have worked through a few stories and have enjoyed recalling some forgotten memories of loving relationships. My accomplishment is that I am learning to know life more intimately. I have learned a lot about myself. Especially that I have made things happen. Thus, the start of this book and the completion of it.

1 *Let's Dine First* *

And who does not like to eat? On a first date with Joseph, my now husband, I was so nervous. I recalled a dinner date, from a few years past, with another fellow that I was wild about.

On our second date Jack took me to a fancy restaurant. I was beside myself with ecstasy. My stomach was in total chaos and sounded like a sawing, grinding, banging dull machine. I don't know if he heard my stomach, but I sure heard it and felt every swallow through my esophagus.

With that memory in mind, I could not go through another meal with a loud gurgling stomach. As we sat down in a restaurant and perused the menu, I looked Joseph in the eyes and flatly stated, "I don't eat."

Wow. Did those words come out of my mouth?

He still married me. He told me later that he could survive on his own if I couldn't cook because he started cooking at the age of nine. With his scientific mind, sequence and precision are essential. For me, every little impromptu cooking disaster turned into a happy learning meal. I tend to work quickly in the kitchen and one morning I forgot to include baking powder in the pancake recipe and then my wrists slipped while pouring the milk. Ooops! Happens a lot when I pour wine or whiskey. Oh well.

Joseph sees this slip of the wrist. "What again? These are not going to turn out."

"So, the batter is thin, so what. I will try it anyway." I am not one to fuss and rather than toss the batter or add more flour, I poured the thin batter into a hot cast iron skillet, added ricotta and creamed cheese, then tossed fresh berries on top. By mistake, I learned to make tasty blintzes.

Cooking skills for one (me) meant small fast meals. Cooking for more than three people meant adjusting portions. Not my forte. Guests usually went home hungry. Too many times I heard the words, "The appetizers were nice. What's the next course?" or "Are there seconds?"

Eating out is usually a treat. A mini-respite from the chores at home and an opportunity to dress up and look your best. There are no two-hour preparations to spend resulting in perhaps a half hour of eating and then another half hour spent cleaning up. The pleasures of dining require a lot of time in preparation and clean up. I learned and easily accepted the best method to organize a party and gather guests is in a restaurant.

Yes, it does take time to research a new restaurant. Will they serve your favorites? Will the steaks be done to perfection and to your taste? The research time is well spent. Plates magically appear and then discreetly are taken away. There is time between courses to digest and enjoy conversation with tablemates or listen to a live band if one is performing.

So very relaxing, no rush. Occasionally there is time to slow down.

Cultural fairs are another way to experience cuisine from around the world. In the fall, our family attended the annual German society's Oktoberfest. We danced on grassy fields to the polka, in time or not, to music performed by oompah-pah bands. Picnic tables were spread throughout the grounds topped with lots of sausages, wursts, and sauerkraut. Many attendees spoke German fluently or at least a few phrases were known. Men wore lederhosen-leather shorts and women wore dirndls-usually a bodice over a white shirt and an apron over a full skirt. Both are traditional Bavarian attire.

Kids were entertained by playing ball, throwing darts, and having the simple joy of just running around.

When we had no money to eat out or no money for transportation, we found a way to experience other parts of the world by learning to make cuisine from various parts of the world, listening to their music, and reading about traditional fabrics and clothing.

I will share some of my favorite dining and gastronomic experiences.

Why Cook? For a Date, Eat it Raw *

Ask not what you can do for your
country. Ask what's for lunch.
Orson Welles

Some of the best chefs and restaurants in New York feature cuisines from all around the world. Without leaving my home city, I was able to enjoy specialty cuisines of Greece, Germany, Israel, Italy, the Caribbean, China, Spain, Mexico, and Korea. Waiters spoke the language of the country the restaurant represented and some wore traditional costumes. I could not afford to travel the world, therefore the next best option to experience another country and satisfy my lust for sensation and taste was to dine at a restaurant featuring authentic cuisine. It was not quite like being in another country, but having a sampling taste of the various cultures, foods, and music left me satisfied.

In my early 20s, I had little money to spend on fancy restaurants. Thankfully, friends and co-workers were willing hosts or sponsors and I was always eager to try new restaurants, especially those with a cosmopolitan or international flare.

A potential amour asked if I would like to lunch at an authentic Japanese restaurant in mid-Manhattan, his treat. Of course I was game to try. I knew nothing about Japanese food and hid my naiveté, "Yes, shall I meet you at the restaurant at noon?"

I had expected the decor to be similar to many other Asian restaurants that I had frequented; however, the storefront immediately revealed otherwise. Unlike other Asian restaurants, which entice potential patrons with photos of over-filled plates of food, there were no pictures nor rubberized dinner replicas in the windows to advertise the cuisine. I had expected, at the very least, a menu to be posted at the entry. There was none. Not a hint of the offerings nor the price. While some Chinese restaurants string a wire of pig's knuckles or roasted fowl hanging by their necks as a curtain and visual menu, here, a simple plain red curtain hid the interior of the restaurant. Inside, the restaurant was sparsely decorated. In traditional zashiki style, there were a few semi-private dining areas separated by a couple of steps and shoji screens.

To my young eyes, this presented as an elegant establishment. Cooking odors were barely detectable. Soft instrumental music played in the background. Conversations from other patrons were in a whisper. I was immediately impressed and thought, "This date has potential."

We were seated at a low table with individual cushions on a woven straw tatami mat. A waitress dressed in a traditional Japanese kimono brought out menus written entirely in one of the styles of Japanese calligraphy. I was willing to try something different or unusual so I did not ask for a translation. I prefer to be surprised as that increases the flow of dopamine and thus the pleasure in dining. The main flavor I cannot tolerate is overly spicy food.

"Is this item spicy?" I asked while pointing to one of the selections.

"No," the waitress responded with an ever so slight sly grin, while bowing her head and stepping back.

"I'll have that," I ordered. Fooling myself, as if I knew what to expect.

My friend Matt knew the menu. He did not translate for me and he ordered his meal.

A medium-sized tray was brought out with what appeared to be bite-sized appetizers. As the tray was brought down to my level...

I saw raw fish. Sashimi, roe, and a side of rice. I took a deep breath.

Now, I must tell you, I have fished, baited my own hooks, cleaned the catch, and definitely cooked all fish prior to eating it.

Although I love fish, I never had an interest in eating it raw and certainly would never eat roe nor anything served as bait on a fishhook.

At least the rice was cooked. I would not leave too hungry. I didn't say a word. Maintaining decorum, I picked up the chopsticks and took the first bite of raw, white fish.

Hmm, not too bad, no odor. Not objectionable, not slimy. Mild flavor. Very clean. Firm, yet tender, and not chewy. With the exception of the roe, I ate everything. The meal was a sampling of about six pieces of sashimi. Having eaten what to me were appetizers for lunch, I left hungry.

Matt and I found our culinary tastes markedly different. While he preferred spicy dishes, I preferred the more bland, core food flavors. It was ironic that our food preferences did not match our personalities. I found him boring and stoic. I was flamboyant and colorful. We soon ended our relationship.

It was not until six years later that Jack, another new boyfriend, would persuade me to try raw oysters.

Jack invited me to a barbecue party on Hood Canal. Other than hearing about the collapse of the Hood Canal Bridge two years prior in 1979, I was not familiar with this body of water. I learned that the canal is a natural fjord, formed by an ice flow thousands of years ago. Over 50 miles in length, the fjord lies between the Olympic and Kitsap Peninsulas. Several commercial oyster farms operate along the shores. A friend of Jack's family-owned waterfront property near the southern legs of the canal with a small oyster bed at the shore. This private shoreline property would be a special treat to see.

The party had already started when we arrived, so we immediately strolled to the backyard on a slightly sloped lawn that led to the shore. Looking past the revelry, between the evergreens and the house, the view to the shore was so serene. A couple of rowboats were floating in placid waters. The only waves to be made would be by rowing. It was a rare sunny day, and I hoped we could take one out.

A few men, with beers in hand, were standing around the barbecue comparing notes on their favorite rubs to put on meat, and the qualities of grills on the market. Another fellow raved about the taste a smoke ring gives. "Yeah, eight hours of smoking. I start in the morning and it is ready by dinnertime with a nice three-quarter inch smoke ring."

"No way, man! Twelve hours and you'll have the most flavorful and juiciest rib."

One fellow cajoled, "Ha! Forget the long wait. Meat is meat. My choice is steak tartare. Why go through the trouble, time, and expense to cook when with minimal prep and cost, the juiciest meats are rare? There are more vitamins and protein in uncooked meat." He flexed his rolling muscles as he selected a raw steak, took a big tearing bite, threw his head back, sucked the dripping red blood, and smacked his lips. Oh, so unappetizing and not for my taste. I grabbed a beer and had my plate ready for a well-cooked burger.

But other partiers could not wait to try the oysters that were freshly taken from the waters' edge. I watched as shells were pried open, revealing large oysters lying in a shimmering liquid of slim. Dipping their tongues into shell crevices, vocal o-o-o-hs and a-a-a-hs were quickly silenced by an oyster slide down their throats, followed by, "Yum, that was awesome!"

"You'll never taste oysters as fresh as these! You have got to try at least one." I was told. "Think of it as your last meal. Perhaps that will make it more palatable," they taunted. Several friends attempted to persuade. "These are not as salty as oysters from the northern shores."

I was repulsed by the look of the oyster and the method of devouring them. My mouth turned down and my facial muscles tightened, simply thinking about placing one even near to my lips.

Yet, I did have to try one. This sliding oyster act was a challenge. I acquiesced, "Alright. I will do it." I could not say 'eat it.' I selected the smallest one I could find, held the cupped side down and slid an oyster knife in near the shell's hinge, then twisted and pushed the knife through. I scraped the oyster out, closed my eyes and swallowed quickly not consuming the liquid. The slide was not too bad. I survived and found oysters to be a superlative aphrodisiac. Jack and I concluded the day with a ride in a rowboat and made some rippled waves.

Over the years since that first oyster slide, I have consumed many oysters of all sizes. Until one day, live worms in a small oyster fixed my delusion, and that was the end of that.

About ten years later, my blue-eyed main man brought me back to eating sushi and sashimi. But, this time, prepared at home. Joseph is quite adept with knives and quick in slicing fish, assembling the layers, rolling, cutting the pieces, and then presenting sushi. It is so lightweight; we can eat two platefuls each. Yum. Raw fish has become the entrée.

Beer Choices

When my family lived in New York, we rarely walked for exercise or recreation. By relocating to Florida, we lived a different lifestyle. My dad was "retired". Meaning that he set his own hours off from his plumbing business. During his time off, we relaxed walking along the docks at marinas. We inhaled deeply the salty smell of the Gulf while being hypnotized by the clanking and ringing of the fishing boats' rigging which were like mythical sirens calling to us, without the gruesome finality. This was our nirvana. After seeing loads of fish being hauled and cleaned, inevitably we would sign up on a charter boat for a day of fishing. Whatever was running, we didn't care. Mostly we fished for mackerel. Some days were dry and we didn't catch a thing.

If our catch was nil we would stop for lunch at one of the popular pubs in Venice, Florida and order fish and chips with a beer. My dad enjoyed light beers. I had a taste for dark beers and one of my favorites was Dortmunder Union. We sat at one of the wooden booths looking out at the docks. A waitress came over immediately, "What will you have?"

"What beers do you have?"

"Oh, we have everything."

"Fantastic. I'll have a Dortmunder Union."

"We don't have that."

"How about a Samuel Smith."

"Nope."

"Well, what do you have?"

"Bud, Michelob, Beck, Heineken..."

My dad interrupted, "I'll have a Heineken."

With no good choice of a beer for me, I ordered a nonmemorable beverage.

Menu Choices

Some of the best dining experiences are made in floating hotels on the sea. Larger cruise ships can hold over 3,000 passengers and over 2,000 crew members! Everything is exquisite and service is a formal affair.

Keeping your weight down can be a struggle between the delectable temptations and then payment by calorie expenditure, it can be difficult to balance. For example, on a typical seven-day cruise, first time guests are flabbergasted by the dining displays and the varied selection of cuisines. There might be three or more restaurants onboard plus a few fast-food stations. Guests will walk through the buffet lanes mindfully salivating over each temptation. What to choose from? What the heck, try at least three per meal.

The first morning on board we are pumped and ready to tour the vessel. First, there is the morning wake-up coffee, enjoyed on an open deck overlooking the sea. An interior café offers a continental treat of quick breads, brioche or croissants. Next, we head to the main dining room for eggs Benedict or a three-egg omelet with oatmeal and bacon on the side. Before lunch, we appraise the buffet and snag a taste or two. The aroma of smoked burgers on an open deck beckons us and is more appealing. After the burger, topped with melted cheese and ketchup, we sink into a lounge chair facing the pool. Several boisterous passengers are boogying around the pool to Caribbean music played by a quartet. Lively conversation ensued with other seated passengers, as we had brought dessert with us. Ice cream sundaes with cake and fruit on the side.

After a couple of hours of discussing site-seeing tours and travel, teatime rolls around about four o'clock. Tea is served with bite-sized cucumber sandwiches, a cheese selection and sweet biscuits. Or, if you are more inclined, before dinner appetizers with a cocktail.

After tea and cocktails, we hurry to our cabin to dress more formally for dinner in the main dining room. Everything on the menu and the waiter described specials sound good. We order a plate for each course. Salad, soup, refreshment, entrée, a second refreshment, and two desserts. Select two, because of the difficulty in deciding on just one.

In addition, during the evening ten p.m. show, servers appear with après champagne, chocolate cherry cordials, and small bite-sized cakes called petit fours.

On day two, we are feeling a little bloated and try to step up the exercise program. This translates to visiting all of the eating venues for each meal. Thereby walking more and stretching my arm out more often to pick up a plate which does indeed expend more calories. Oh, that vanilla crème Brule was so vainly creamy and easily slid down my throat.

As the days go on, we become a little more selective in where we eat. We have determined our favorite eating places and favorite servers. The walking program is not helping to work off calories, so we have cut back on second helpings and swim a few more laps in the pool.

By day six, the day before our last, I lament going home and do not look forward to eating the uninspired boring display of meals that we prepare. We start thinking about what can be brought back home. An extra roll and dessert get stuffed into a handbag. We order a second dinner in the cabin and place the meal into plastic bags.

At the last morning breakfast meal, everything looks appetizing. We see guests packing croissants and other transportable foods into their suitcases.

"Too bad our suitcases cannot hold one more item. I gained only two pounds on this cruise," I proudly comment while squinting towards the buffet.

"Go for it!" Joseph chuckles, "We have 15 more minutes before disembarkation. A second helping of eggs and sausage won't hurt your figure. I'll sit with the suitcases. While you are at the buffet, bring back a Belgian waffle."

Fitting The Dress Celebrity
Entrée or Not

Seize the moment. Remember all those
women on the 'Titanic' who waved off
the dessert cart. – Erma Bombeck

For formal nights, my husband and I had picked out an extravagant black silky evening gown at Macy's Department store. A horizontally ribbed corselet on top made to be tightly fit to mid-hip. A huge bow at the back hip line led down to a short train. It had fit me perfectly.

Two years later we booked a seven-day cruise to Alaska. A week before the cruise I tried on all the outfits I was going to wear. A few pounds had been added to my slender figure, and when I tried on the evening gown, I held my breath. Even so, the zipper would not close. My beautiful dress! I could not and would not do without. A required strict diet was on order, even though it was too late to lose the minimal poundage to comfortably wear the one formal dress in my closet. Of course, I packed it anyway and maintained a strict diet during the whole seven-day cruise. That gown was going to fit and be worn on formal night.

My dinner selections were small. I picked my favorite small portion menu items and restricted the meals to no more than two courses. Either soup and salad or if the dessert was not to be missed, then an appetizer and a dessert. Or I might eat a small portion of a full-sized serving and my husband would finish the rest. He had expandable pants.

Customary social form was to order all of the courses and ask for seconds. Moderation in portions was quite out of the norm for cruise ship dining. During our first dinner in the main dining room, the waiters watched me closely. They shifted from one leg to the other, walked around the serving station, and waited for dining orders. Receiving none they offered alternative dishes trying to please me. They seemed to be very protective that I might waste away to a pencil thin waist. Inevitably, the waiter would inquire, "Does the lady not care for the meal?" They would again offer suggestions for items that were not on the menu. My husband would repeat, "No she is fine. She does not eat much." Until finally, he motioned to his waist in an hourglass form. The waiter quietly nodded and understood. Some of the newer waiters to our table were also beside themselves. As they stood between tables, we could hear, "How is it that she does not eat?" Our waiter then in turn explained to the servers not to ask further.

I ate slowly to keep pace with the three or four courses my husband was eating. Since it takes about 20 minutes for the stomach to tell the brain that there is food in the digestive tract, eating slowly was actually a benefit, which prevented overindulgence.

Yes, I was hungry during the whole cruise and coveted every plate I saw. For my dieting efforts, only two pounds were lost that week, but at least I wore that gown.

Entrée

On the other end of the spectrum are the gourmands who eat two or three times as much as they normally do and may gain ten percent more in weight. Unlike most cruisers, my husband has some good control and does not overindulge very often. He is a meat and some potato person. One of his favorite cuts of beef is prime rib. During our first dinner on one cruise, my husband relished the juicy prime rib. Our wonderful and efficient waiter asked, "Would you like another?"

Oh, did Joseph's eyes ever light up. "Oh, yes please."

Another plate was brought, sans the potato.

For every dinner thereafter, the waiter asked the same question many times.

A Second Cocktail?

Smaller cruise ships are so worth the extra cost over the large floating hotels that try to pass as cruise ships. While we certainly enjoy traveling on the larger ships, and saving money; the large ships carry too many passengers for the stewards to know each passenger's preferences and sailing history.

On a small ship, wait staff indulge guests with extra pampering and personalized service. Upon boarding, photo identification is given to staff who are immediately coached in each passenger's preferences, desires and past voyages. Joseph and I treated ourselves to a seven-day cruise aboard a 200-passenger vessel served by 105 crew members.

The bar manager, Michael, had served us on previous cruises and he appreciated our tastes and knowledge of the various liquors available onboard. An invitation was then extended to join him and his assistant manager for a vintage Port tasting in the lounge.

Upon entering the lounge, we looked for other guests. To our surprise, this was an exclusive tasting as only four of us occupied the lounge. He poured a line-up of twenty to sixty-year-old Ports. Not surprisingly, we favored the sixty-year-old Port, but unfortunately, we would not ever buy one as they are way above our price range.

As a special treat, Michael introduced us to Madeira, a dry fortified wine with a nutty acidic flavor. Only wine made and grown on the volcanic island of Madeira can use the Madeira name. Ten-year and older bottles quickly became my favorite after-dinner drink accompanied by a bite of dark chocolate. Oh paradise. A full-bodied Madeira sipped, lining my mouth and then a bite of chocolate slowly melting to carry the wine down. Lovely.

We enjoyed sunny weather all week during the voyage along the Mediterranean coastline from Nice, France to Barcelona, Spain. Later that week we ordered champagne from the bar on the sports deck. Taking glass in hand we entered the hot tub after acknowledging Michael's warnings of high heat increasing the effects of alcohol and reading signs by the tub which included "No glass", and health warnings relating to heat and heart conditions.

On a larger cruise ship, we were once told to vacate the tub and finish our drinks at the bar! The cruise line did not want any liability to risk a lawsuit. But here, guests are treated as owners and their preferences are honored. No reprimands disturbed us as the water jets massaged our muscles.

The champagne sparkled like diamonds in the sun's rays. We savored each sip not wanting to finish the pour, nor did we want to leave the tub for a second glass. Joseph finished his first tubular glass and placed it on the side rail of the tub. No more than thirty seconds passed when Michael appeared with a freshly filled glass and whisked the empty away. Now, that is service.

These are the experiences enjoyed exclusively on select smaller vessels. The upfront economical outlay can be banked in long-term held special memories. It is like wearing expensive silk shirts that can last a lifetime, softly caressing your skin and may bring fun experiences, unlike inexpensive everyday polyester which will have to be replaced and forgotten several times in a lifetime, and overall will ultimately cost more.

No Choices?

When touring, the search for a restaurant that is acceptable to Joseph is a painful experience. The hunt requires walking for over an hour, reading several posted menus, peaking into the restaurant to observe the clientele and wait staff, and possibly checking a restaurant inspection website, if a computer is available.

On one such scouting tour in London, we passed a Greek restaurant that appeared not quite open for dinner. The front door was open and the room empty except for the waiters that were bustling about. Joseph went through his checklist and was not sold on eating there due to lack of customers.

There was no wait line as is typical for-in his determination-an acceptable restaurant. An hour later, with no decision made as yet, I was famished and insisted that we go back to the Greek restaurant. As we entered, the manager stopped us, "I'm sorry, we are closed for a private wedding dinner this evening." Ah! Thus the reason for no customers.

I must have looked famished and Joseph exasperated and dejected because the manager said sympathetically, "We can help. We have about a half hour before guests arrive."

"Yes! Thank you very much. We can eat within that time frame!"

Thanks to this understanding restaurant owner, we enjoyed one of the best Greek cuisines we have ever tasted.

French Bistro

Although food is a common language worldwide, it is beneficial to know a few words and customs prior to visiting a country where English is not the primary language. In preparation for our trip to Europe, Joseph took a course on basic French and I brushed up on Spanish.

In Paris, France, we had an hour and a half to spare before our train departure, and being hungry we entered a café near the Gare de Lyon.

The menu was in French and the waiter addressed us in French. I nodded and Joseph asked me, "What did he say?"

I leaned forward, shrugged, and whispered, "I have no idea." We resumed helping each other with the menu. The waiter returned and spoke in French. Joseph tried unsuccessfully to interpret so I replied in English giving my order. Joseph had more time to think; he recouped and gave his order in French.

The waiter checked back with us a couple of times always speaking in French and I always in English.

Joseph was desperately trying to analyze the words spoken. He was perplexed, "What did he say?"

I translated the waiter's words.

"How do you know? How did you interpret?"

"I focused on facial expression and mannerism. I trusted that waiters worldwide ask the same questions at specific times during a meal."

The waiter and I spoke the common language of food and service.

Spice it up?

I was raised on plain American food. My taste buds have not been taxed by hot, overly spicy food. I can taste the sweetness in carrots, the overly acidic tones of citrus, and the tart bitterness in some celery. In season, fresh unspiced food is delicious. My mother hardly used any salt, minimal pepper, and no onions nor garlic. She had pureed all my baby food that consisted of fruits and vegetables. So, I grew up loving broccoli, peas, and almost all of the green vegetables that even some gourmands will not eat.

When cooking for guests, I add flavor by pureeing vegetables to thicken soups and add a wine to side dishes. An orange liqueur added to sautéed carrots adds sweetness. Guests can sprinkle crystallized colorful finishing salts if desired. These salts do have a flavor and come in various colors: gray, black, or pink.

As a teenager, I was introduced to pizza and had a taste for garlic. It infused my pores. I loved it, as did my dad. My mother abhorred the odor and taste.

One summer my mother and I were touring Europe and for some reason, she chose an Indian restaurant in Brussels for one dinner. An unusual choice, possibly recommended by the hotel concierge. I do not know, as I was 12 and ate where she ate. Anyway, neither of us had ever eaten Indian food.

Oh my. Tears ran down my eyes and my face was moist with perspiration throughout the whole meal. Needless to say, the food was overly spicy for me. I do not remember what the dishes were. Many years later in my late twenties, I tried Indian food again. Milder dishes, which I found to be very tasty. Sweet fragrant Jasmine rice is lovely and yogurts cool the hot spices from my palate.

Not finding a good Indian restaurant in Seattle that was acceptable to my tastes led me to take a couple of Indian cooking classes through the University of Washington Extension program in 1981. According to friends, the resulting meals turned out much better and tastier than those made by professional cooks.

Desserts

Cakes are healthy too; you just eat a small slice. – Mary Berry

Salt, sugar, and fat. These are some elements that food companies add to processed foods in mass quantities. Many people are addicted to one or more of these discretionary additives. Even with 10,000 taste buds, salt, lard, and most fats have zero flavor to me.

Joseph and I were winding down from a care-free two-week Club Med vacation. We were waiting in a hot and humid airport on one of the Polynesian islands for our return flight to the States.

I was impatient, sweating my brains out, and thirsty. Not a pretty appearance for the last day of our honeymoon. A big sign depicted one of my favorite cooling sweets and I was drawn to it. I purchased a single soft-serve vanilla ice cream and took the first lick of wonderful creamy texture.

Hmm. Odd taste. My second thought was, is ice cream made differently in Tahiti or could this be made with a soymilk base? Back home, when I diet, I employ mind over matter. Plain yogurt becomes sour cream, and vanilla yogurt becomes my favorite 'ice cream' dessert. So, it was not a far stretch that I imagined the ice cream was made of something other than milk.

"Here taste this." I shoved the now dripping soft serve toward his lips. Not being able to resist, he bent to lick the cone.

I blurted out, "I think it's bad."

He already had a taste and recoiled, "That's sour. I would never have bought ice cream here."

"Gee, thanks for warning me."

He has not let me live down that experience.

We never asked if sour ice cream was the ingredient used in Tahiti. Since this was an open-air airport, catering to tourists, we did not want to take a chance and into the garbage went the ice cream.

But to get back to the dining experience on cruise ships... The chefs prepare unique dishes with precise presentations and colorful, extravagant table displays. Each meal can be prepared to order and any allergy or specific request for a special meal or ingredient is given personal attention.

On one particular cruise during a flu season, we estimated that at least half of the passengers had a flu, a cold, or some such virus.

There is deep belief and scientific evidence to support a theory that there are beneficial chemicals in garlic to not only increase one's immunity but also to stave off viruses and germs, and possibly close contact with humans due to the odor that some find objectionable. The opposing beliefs and scientific evidence are that over-the-counter medication is what works to fend off viruses and that garlic is simply a placebo that is best used to increase flavors in a meal. I subscribe to both arguments.

Copper is another antimicrobial substance, which is beneficial to our health when water pipes are made of copper, and many handrails and faucets are made of copper plate.

Toward the end of one of our dinners in the main dining room, we were determined to order dessert. Not being able to decide between an apple pie or a fruit soufflé, I gave up, altered my thinking, and decided on giving my immunity a boost by ordering garlic cloves.

The waiter asked, "How would you like that prepared?"

I responded, "Only a few cloves on a plate."

"Do you mean raw?"

"Yes," I stated matter-of-factly. He then softened his questioning look, took everyone's order and immediately walked briskly to the kitchen.

We continued our dinner conversation until the desserts arrived. With the waiter off to my side, outside of my vision, he seemed to present my 'dessert' unpretentiously; however, my tablemates later mentioned that the waiter had returned with great flare and had ceremoniously placed that white plate with doily, in the center of my place setting. He pulled back to observe while two busboys stood grinning behind him. I was quite pleased with the dish, but my tablemates erupted in laughter. Perhaps the waiter may have perceived this as a joke?

How was that first taste of a clove? Delicious! The waiter actually stood to the side to check if the dish was to my satisfaction. The second taste? Even better with the delicate hint of parsley sprigs garnishing three cloves of garlic. The plump clove was mild, like a warm savory smooth mustard flavor. I believe this dining service experience made the waiters' evening.

And the garlic worked its magic! While I did not contract any sniffles, my tablemates who had laughed at my dessert choice, all came down with bad colds. Also, the wait staff never questioned my unusual dinner requests again.

2 *Work Off Those Calories*

Hula Whoo-Hoo!

There are many activities to be involved in on a cruise ship. The more a body moves and participates in energetic movement, the more one can partake in dining experiences.

Showtime was 50s night in the disco and the host challenged the audience to try keeping a hula hoop up. Most everyone, including myself, had one in grade school. Many years have passed since I played that game.

I typically do not volunteer to be on stage, and in this instance, I was happy to watch.

"Oh, go on! You are good at this. You wowed the Tahitians, dancing ote'a[1] with your hips shaking. Give it a whirl!" Joseph continued to praise, "You are the best!"

Oh, who could resist the compliment? As I had done in Tahiti, I pulled his arm, "Come up with me."

Joseph shook his head. He laughed and on this occasion would not budge.

I was in for it. This would be a challenge on a ship when unexpected rolls might throw you off balance. But I was

---

[1] Ote'a (otea) is a traditional Tahitian dance with rapid hip-shaking keeping up with very fast percussion beats.

sure-footed on vessels. Other participants might not be so lucky. So I had a better chance of centralizing my balance to keep my footing and maintain the circular momentum to keep the hoops in place.

Each participant received one hoop to start. As the hoops dropped and contestants left the stage, another hoop would be added to our torsos. Soon there were only four of us on stage. I had to keep the momentum going. And I did. We were told to keep moving around the stage as we twirled the five or six hoops around our torsos. I made small steps to keep the hoops up. Now only two of us. I could hear the crowd cheering and music in the background. The other female contestant gave me a nasty look. She tried to come close to me to knock my hoops down. Close enough that I heard the hoops slide and knock against each other. I took a few steps away. I concentrated harder, moved faster and harder. Although all sounds became muffled, I heard the announcer yelling, but I didn't understand one word. I was in my body, in tune with the hoops feeling each one bounce off me.

The hoops circled from my breasts down to my thighs. I didn't count them; I kept up the rapid momentum with firm torso and hip movements. Finally, the other contestant lost her momentum and hoops. I kept going. The host stopped me! For my efforts, the prizes kept coming. All small souvenirs from the ship, like a t-shirt, drinking glasses and accoutrements, notepads, sun visor and more.

When I returned to the table, Joseph was beaming. A fun night was remembered by guests for the next few days. Many guests stopped to chat about the hula contest while I power-walked the promenade. I continued to burn off calories by walking, swimming, and dancing in order to indulge in the fantastic cuisine.

Thirty-two years later, another opportunity presented itself in another hula contest. I had overindulged at the retiree luncheon buffet and needed to move. With no reluctance I was on stage with a few other contestants. We were all about the same retirement age.

This time there was one hoop each, and three rounds, plus a practice set. The hoops fell quickly on all of us! But I did win all three rounds, which in caloric count made up for the second helping of pulled pork.

Sea Bubbles *

Life, forms, and colors underwater are amazing. Have you been there? Colors so vibrant they are iridescent. By actually diving or snorkeling in the oceans, you will see how different the underwater sea world is from shallow aquariums. Even though my eyesight uncorrected is 20/300, I am not so blind under the sea. The water magnifies all sea life. Fish, plants, and coral all seem about one-third larger than they actually are.

Magnification, however; did not bring objects into focus nor make objects appear any closer for me. Due to my bad eyesight, any object more than three feet away appeared fuzzy. I was quite apprehensive to be further than arm's length from my partner. In fact, I held tightly to his hand throughout my first experience snorkeling in Tahiti. He tried to help by pointing out various fish, crustaceans, and sea turtles. Brightly colored fish stood out against the overall light blue water and pale tan sand. Unfortunately, squinting didn't help. If the objects' colors were in muted shades of sand or grey, I could barely decipher outlines. Anything further than three feet away appeared to be simply the movements of shadows.

We snorkeled in shallow waters, in the mornings and in the afternoons, for hours at a time. Thus, slowly, I became a bit more comfortable and self-confident in the water. My eyes no longer the size of saucers and no longer needing to grip my partners hand, I agreed to try drift snorkeling. Our tour guide led a group of us, two each in four rowboats, out to a spot where he said we would see sharks.

We lowered ourselves into the warm water and drifted effortlessly with the current. Little exertion was needed as we floated in calm and smooth waters. About 30 to 50 feet below us, near the bottom of the sea, were many sharks swimming in the same direction as we were. Our bodies cast shadows on the sea floor. I am sure they were aware of us above. Without vision correction, it was difficult to identify the species, as their outlines were hardly discernible. The telltale signs that they were sharks were the outline of their dark pectoral fins and their steady tail side movements propelling them forward. I estimated they were about five to six feet in length. As long as the sharks stayed at that level, all would be fine.

As we headed back to the boat, Joseph rapidly swam past me. He swung his leg over the rail and got into the rowboat rather quickly. Then in a low-pitched clear voice, out of character, yelled, "Give me your hand!" His face revealed no sign of distress yet he pulled me up with a sharp tug and then pointed out to the waters behind me. I turned to look, in time to see a shark about ten feet from the boat swimming towards me. As my legs were now in the boat and there would be no snack, it quickly turned away as it swam back down.

"Why didn't you tell me?"

"He was following you. I didn't want you to panic and flail."

Close call, I thought.

All other snorkeling outings were relatively safe in protected inlets. One other close call occurred in Bora Bora, Tahiti as we were holding hands walking along on a deserted beach at the water's edge. Joseph was on the waterside and I was next to him upland. The water lapped at our ankles as the gentle waves flowed up the beach. There was a soft breeze that cooled the humid ninety-degree heat. This being our honeymoon, romance was on Joseph's mind and on my mind as well. I hoped that we might find an area curtained by tall shrubs for a private afternoon interlude.

My mind was filled with fantasies of our bodies intertwined standing in a surround of scented frangipani, jasmine shrubs, and shaded by coconut-palm trees. However, as a multi-tasker, my eyes were constantly alternating between the upland beach area-where the vendors were selling hats and trinkets-to scanning the sandy beach; and the expanse of open sea to the horizon.

I felt so free. Free from work pressures, free from inhaling polluted air, free from the stares and judgments of strangers, free from the constant noise from machines, lawn mowers, barking dogs, and conversations. I barely felt the earth under my feet.

Joseph gave a slight tug on my hand. Slowly and increasing in volume at each word, "Are you listening to me?" entered my ears and registered in my brain.

"I have never seen a beach without people. Ummh yes, of course, I am listening to you."

I didn't have time to get more words out. Quickly, with all my strength, I pulled Joseph away from the water's edge. His body slightly stiffened and with a creased brow questioned, "What the heck?"

I pointed to three sharks' dorsal fins that were visible above the water's surface, their denticles giving a velvety appearance below the surface as they were swimming quickly towards us. Then in water too shallow and with pectoral fins in the sand the sharks quickly turned back to the sea. When he saw them and realized the unexecuted attack, he began to shake a bit. Taking a big breath, he brought his hand up to his forehead, smoothed his hair, and he let out a big sigh of relief, "Whoa, how did you see them?"

"You know me; I always try to take in everything that is around me."

Taking big breaths, he again sighed with relief, "If you hadn't stopped me, I would have been bitten!"

"Never mind that, they might have pulled you out to sea! It is hard to believe that sharks could swim in shallow water not covering their backs."

We never did find a secluded area.

Although I missed seeing details of the undersea world, my first snorkeling vacation was exhilarating and a revelation. Fish make a lot of noise. I found the sounds underwater to be muffled. Fizzy soft-drink sounds. Soft little crunching sounds of teeth grinding away at coral. Ticking and pecking clatter, some almost like a woodpecker pecking a tree, or the call of a grackle. Some sounds were like a soft foghorn. The whoosh of waves. The clatter was incredible and noisy. Not loud, but a symphonic undertone.

* * *

In order to expand my experience to another level in the ocean, Joseph suggested that I take a diving course, become certified, and get prescription goggles.

On our second snorkeling vacation, I was still without prescription goggles. We were in Cancun, Mexico in an inlet where the fish were protected. Unafraid, the fish swam close and seemed to be as curious about snorkelers as we were about marine life. We always wore gardening-type gloves to protect our hands and fingers from cuts and abrasions. My gloves had little colored flowers. We usually had some peas to feed the fish, but this time I didn't have peas and pointed my finger at a clown fish *(Amphiprioninae)* that was curious and staring at me. He quickly darted and before I could pull back the 'Clown' bit the tip of my finger! I shivered from that bite, as chills ran through my arms to my shoulders and down my torso. I was shocked and taken aback by that sudden darting movement. Luckily, no blood was lost as the glove provided the needed barrier.

Waters had been calm on all of our previous outings. I felt more confident and no longer needed to hold Joseph's hand. With his hands free and unhampered by mine, he had brought his underwater video camera. On replay, he could show me what I had not been seeing. We were now snorkeling off the beaches with surf ending in frothy foam. On our return to shore, waves were breaking over a reef. Joseph advised, "Now you have to time your swim so that you are over the reef as the wave comes. You do not want to get slammed down and cut up on the coral." I nodded my understanding.

He swam off ahead of me and about three feet to the right. His eyes were in the viewfinder intent upon capturing video. I followed and waited a moment for the next wave, which surged as I was above the reef and carried me safely away. The tide was coming in. What I did not realize was that there would be an angle to the current pushing me to the right and closer to Joseph and soon I was directly behind him. He did not detect that I was behind him. I am a lightweight, not a strong swimmer and even in normal circumstances, cannot keep up with him. I smiled inwardly, "Ha. Ha. I caught up to him and may get to shore first." A larger wave came, brought my light body up, and then after the crest, slammed me down hard. The turbulence of the water stirred up the bottom limiting visibility. I flailed, kicked, and tried to angle away from him to no avail. The current was too strong for me. Now, I like to be on top of Joseph, but this was not the right moment. We were then in about two feet of water. My slam brought Joseph down into the sand, camera in the sand, and me on top of him. With the snorkel in my mouth, I couldn't warn him.

Back at home, I made it a priority to get fitted for prescription goggles and take a scuba diving course to improve my snorkeling abilities. Although Joseph was a certified diver, he decided to join the class to be supportive as my diving buddy. The course consisted of a couple of hours of in-classroom instruction, then some practice in a pool in the Seattle neighborhood of Ballard. Understanding the basics was the beginning of feeling a little more confident.

I kept up and advanced to the open watercourse in Alki Beach. The instructor didn't take us into deep water, which was fine with me, as my ears do not clear easily when moving through different atmospheric pressures. Several different techniques are needed before my ears clear. A bit of swallowing or blowing my nose, or tilting of the head. Thus, I was always last in resurfacing.

For the final open water exam, we dove at Brackett's Landing, adjacent and north of the Edmonds Ferry terminal. Puget Sound waters are a bit chilly year-round. After the initial shock of cold water seeping through the wrist, ankle, and neck openings of the wet suit, the water acts as insulation. That thin layer of water warming to near body temperature can become quite warm while swimming underwater.

Brackett's Landing is a Marine Preserve and Sanctuary, providing a home to octopuses, crabs, sea cucumbers, and anemones. But we were not there to see the marine life and shipwrecks. We were to scale down a piling. The weather was with us as the waters were calm. As I slowly descended, air bubbles from my oxygen tank swirled around me. Visibility was not good in the churned-up murky waters and I could not see any of the other divers. The sounds, of a horn's blast and the ferry's engine rumbling, ready to leave for Bainbridge Island, temporarily took my mind away from the swirling bubbles that gurgled to the surface. I held tightly to the piling and stopped several times to clear my ears. Oohhh, the swirling of bubbles put me into vertigo. At about a 20-foot descent I could not go any further. Holding tighter to the piling and shutting my eyes, telling myself that my body was not spinning as that would be impossible while holding onto a stationary piling. After a few minutes of concentrated thought, the sensation abated and sensibilities set in. Setting my mind straight, I opened my eyes knowing that the air bubbles in motion caused the vertigo and not a body movement.

Finally, I descended to the required 40-foot depth, surfaced, passed the course, and obtained a PADI certification

(Professional Association of Diving Instructors). I was pleased that I had finished something that I had started even though it was uncomfortable and on one dive a forced fast ascent caused an ear to bleed. Getting out of the dive suit and having redressed, I announced to Joseph, "I will never do that again."

"I am really proud of you for finishing. Even if you never go scuba diving, you will find that snorkeling will be much easier."

I was ready and eager to go back to snorkeling in the tropics. Wow, my skills improved tremendously from my first experience in Tahiti. I knew that I would be comfortable and confident on future snorkeling swims. Plus, I could see 20/20 magnified with the new prescription goggles!

* * *

Ke'e Beach on the island of Kauai is near the end of Kuhio Highway on the north side of the island and before reaching the Na Pali coast and trailhead. Parking is very limited. Today, reservations and shuttle buses are required, but in the 1990s, reservations were not heard of. We parked in a small cleared area, crossed a river and a road to walk to a reef protected beach.

I pointed out sea turtles gliding through the water before Joseph saw them. Grays no longer faded into shadows and every little bubble and detritus were visible.

In Ixtapa, Mexico, while packing for an afternoon of deep water snorkeling, Joseph handed a boot knife to me. "Here, strap this around your thigh."

"Oh, cool! What do I need that for?"

"The boat will take us out to the sea cliffs where I'll be diving the wall with the other passengers. The tour guide will let you off in a snorkeling area first. You will have to be wary of unfamiliar boats coming in close to you. And maybe you can spear a fish or two for dinner?" he smiled.

While Joseph dove the sea cliffs, I snorkeled alone in murky deep water. Visibility was tarnished due to effluence being discharged into the water from boats and towns. Protective eye goggles and the snorkel kept the sewage out. If other vacationers were snorkeling and hadn't gotten sick, I would continue snorkeling. But, I would not swim at the beach where the direct outwash flowed. That would have been too gross.

The highlight of this swim was seeing a barracuda which hovered motionless inches below the surface of the water. At first, I hoped it might be dead. Seeing clearly with the prescription glasses, I did not have to get closer to investigate. Its fins barely moved, and its eyes looked lifeless. It hung horizontally as though suspended as a mobile while particles floated and swirled around it. Smaller fishes stayed away and I retreated slowly as well and remembered to stay calm.

After the swim, I was eager to hear about Joseph's dive down the wall. "Was the water clear further out? What type of fish did you see?"

Joseph was disgusted by the discharges. "I won't come back here. The water was murky. I even saw toilet paper floating by us. It's unbelievable that in this populated touristy area that the sewage is not treated or diverted elsewhere."

A year later we returned to Hawaii and snorkeled in a lagoon where a bluehead wrasse stayed on my leg for hours cleaning away. If the fish mistook me for another fish that must have meant that my swimming abilities had really improved.

Of all the snorkeling trips, Tahiti was my first and the most colorful venue. I am so pleased and elated to have experienced the undersea environment.

Not only practice and persistence but having the right equipment and training improved and enhanced these snorkeling adventures.

Modesty Takes a Ride *

"This is the dullest and dumbest mind-numbing faux sport I have ever seen. Standing still, holding on to a rope, while being towed behind a motorboat. How boring is that? What kind of skill set is needed, if any?" I rhetorically asked Joseph. Disinterested, I rolled my eyes and continued, "Let's go snorkeling!" I expected that Joseph would agree as I gently prodded him in the direction of another beach for an anticipated afternoon of snorkeling.

Joseph and I were vacationing on Bora Bora in Tahiti. I was in my 30s and physically fit. Among other activities, we enjoyed racing sailboats, downhill and cross-country skiing, and ice-skating. We participated in sports that required a higher level of physical and mental self-control and I knew my capabilities.

Joseph lowered the bar, "Oh come on now, if you can stand upright and raise a leg, you can water-ski," he cajoled in response to my poke. "It's not like scuba diving, and much easier than downhill skiing. You can at least try this and be successful with one run around this little lagoon."

That last comment was a challenge. With a heavy sigh, my chest deflated and I gave in. "For you, I will try this boring activity."

From a dockside float, I watched the others go before me and I quickly assessed how to put the skis on, how to hold the tow bar, and what form the body should take whilst the boat accelerated bringing one's body up from staying afloat to a standing position.

Easy peasy. Yes, I can stand upright to give this a try. The brief instruction from the driver was, "Keep your ski tips up out of the water."

In the water, I held onto the tow bar, as the boat accelerated quickly pulling me up. The force from the velocity put some pressure on my sporty arthritic hips. A weight like I was carrying an 80-pound sack. Still, easy peasy. Nothing to do. That heavyweight sensation was overridden by the wind blowing water droplets off my skin while I scanned the shoreline to see where Joseph was. As the boat accelerated and rounded a curve, I thought, "He better be watching my fluid moves."

I could no longer hold my thighs close enough together to keep my swim suit up. I then let out a scream as the weight of the water pulled my bikini bottom down to my ankles. Embarrassment overcame me being seen in that state. A dilemma arose.

Did I continue the exhilarating ride while giving everyone the extra show or cut the show short and hope that few onlookers saw what happened?

Modesty overcame me as I held on for a short time and then let go. Relieved, I slowly descended into the water.

Would I try this sport again, and wear a one-piece bathing suit instead? Highly unlikely as I'd rather have more control over my destination. To lead and not follow. Although, I have to admit that the exhilarating euphoria of speed was fun and similar to the effect of being on a ride in an amusement park. The thrill of that short waterskiing ride was worth having the experience - once.

Skiing *

Watch and Learn - Mom

One winter when I was about nine years old, my father decided that we should try a new sport. We were vacationing in the Catskills and there was a bunny hill ski slope behind the hotel. Downhill ski equipment was provided by the hotel. The conditions were just right for beginners. The sun was bright reflecting the grooves carved by previous skiers into the foot-deep semi-powdery snow. He led the way on the first short successful run and then showed me how to grab the towline to be pulled back up the hill.

At the end of the afternoon my dad asked, "You did really well. How did you like your day?"

"I didn't fall once! I had the most fun being pulled uphill by the towrope."

For first-timers, I thought that we did quite well. No falls, no pain. We both had a successful day.

My parents were hoping for a multi-talented daughter that might become a star in some capacity or another or a daughter that would excel in a sport and compete in the Olympics. Although skating professionally was not in my future, I became proficient in ice skating and passed the pre-gold test. Many years of ballet and gymnastics improved my form on the ice.

I dabbled in many sports, including basketball, tennis, swimming, and field and ice hockey. I was fairly athletic so when my parents bought a pair of downhill Head skis and leather-lined Nordic boots for me I was quite ecstatic. Remembering the positive experience on the bunny hill in the Catskills, I was eager to engage in a new activity where there would be no pressing lessons and no pressure to be the next Ingemar

Stenmark. Skiing would be a fun extracurricular sport. I would enjoy choreographing freestyle moves without a set pattern.

In the 1960s and 1970s, the ski length was determined by your height. Arm up; hand down; measure from the floor to the palm and that would be the length of your skis. In most instances, this length is probably two feet longer than what is recommended today.

I was not a dare-devil athlete. I was actually quite timid and cautious when learning how to ski. I took my self-lessons quite seriously. Repetition was key for muscle memory and control. I sidestepped the bunny hill for about half the day and alternated with the towrope when bored with sidestepping. Through scrutinizing the moves of other skiers and watching the ski instructors, I learned and mastered the basic ski maneuvers and eventually over the years became adept at skiing moguls.

My imagination as to what skiing should entail were ahead of my time. Unfortunately, I didn't have the creativity or the know-how to invent products, but I dreamed of short skis. Short skis would enable quick turns and kicks. Wouldn't it be great fun to perhaps perform ballet moves on the slope?

That skiing style would not become mainstream until the 1980s. Ski ballet was popular in the 1970s and the 1980s. Freestyle skiing, a different category, became recognized in 1979. In 1980, FIS Freestyle Ski World Cup arranged freestyle competitions.

Look Like a Pro – Is it Style or Ability that Matters?

As late as the mid-1980s, I still had my first skis and boots from the 1960s. The boot's buckles were becoming stiff and difficult to work. It took a great deal of force to push them down. On first dates, the boys were always incredulous that I asked for help in closing the buckles. A few were surprised and embarrassed that they too struggled and had to put more effort and weight into it.

I took after my dad in regards to frugality. It was not necessary to buy a new pair, because the old ones worked fine as did my 20-year-old black ski pants and fluffy tan, five dollar, balloon-shaped ski jacket. No style here. I could ski.

Snoqualmie and Hyak were an easy 40-minute drive on I-90 from Seattle. The close proximity was perfect for a last-minute decision to ski for a single day or an evening, and allowed the opportunity to ski several times during the winter. After a few seasons, I still skied the intermediate slopes and had not yet mastered the moguls. My friend Rick and I enjoyed evening runs at Snoqualmie. He was a better skier than I was and always encouraged me to ski more moguls. On one run, I had the idea to show off a bit, but Rick had gotten ahead of me. He would miss seeing my run. I needed to hurry in order to catch up with him. *Damn the torpedoes and ski at full speed straight down the hill,* I told myself. I kept my knees loose trying to minimize friction on the snow and the lift helped with speed. I was in the zone of hearing only the skis skimming the crystals on the snow, and my body structure flowing in response to every slight bump and depression of the slope. Like a slinky, I felt lighter than air.

It was a bit dark and the spotlights were on, so I missed seeing a mogul. Too late, my ski tips moved to the rise of an invisible mogul. Up in the air I went. Oh, how embarrassing. I had to close my eyes. All sounds evaporated. *I'm going to fall flat on my face,* and I waited for the face plant. At some point, without quite knowing what had happened, as I opened my eyes, sounds were becoming apparent again. I realized that I was still skiing facing downhill on my two skis, and not as I had expected to be lying on my side buried in the snow. Then I heard applause, cheering, and whooping. I turned my head toward the ski lift and riders were raising their arms and pointing at me. Really? What did I do? I felt exhilarated. No cameras would tell the tale. Later my skiing partner told me I had gone head down, skis overhead, and completed a 360-degree flip. That might have been the start of my ballet on the slopes.

No one taught me that. I had never seen someone else do that in person to emulate the somersault. Other than cartwheels, I had never been upside down and certainly never in mid-air without a lifeline. I had always been too cautious and rigid to execute moves that I determined were beyond my capabilities.

There is some truth in Edgar Degas words, "Only when he no longer knows what he is doing does the painter do good things." That is why I live the chaotic life.

Relax! Don't hold back. Stretching my limits to learn something new every day, I love it.

I continued to ski casually without overextending my capabilities. My comfort level changed a few years later, when my fiancé, Joseph, a former ski instructor who liked to ski fast, was anxious to improve my form and get me on the more advanced runs. You know, push me and extend my capabilities to keep up with him on the expert slopes. Under his guidance, I quickly mastered the moguls.

He was also concerned with style. He hated my beige and brown (what he called Doberman dog colored) puffy ski jacket. In addition, my 20-year-old boots should be replaced.

He tried to convince me. The buckles on new boots would be easy to close and the new lining material would keep my feet warm. And with better equipment, my style and capabilities would improve. His chorus was, "I am sick and tired of hearing about your frozen feet and fed up with struggling to help you clamp your boots. I am not going to do it anymore. I'd rather ski."

The old leather lined boots did little to insulate and I worked with mind over matter. Mental pictures of fireplaces and warm sunny backyards helped to make me feel less cold. Non-ski images were however a bit distracting and the struggle to close my boots took a few minutes time away from being on the slope. So, I slowly gave in. I bought a new slim styled jacket, at a surplus store for fifteen dollars. At that price, there was a tear on the back. The tear was easily mended and I decorated the whole back with ski patches from various resorts. (Thanks Dad, for the frugality tips!) Joseph surprised me at Christmas with new boots. They were wonderful. The buckles on the new boots were easy to close and the foam lined material kept my feet warm. My skiing technique did improve and we skied in style on the expert slopes at Big Mountain in Montana.

* * *

Back in New York in the mid-1970s, I first tried cross-country on a rented pair of skis. The movements were similar to walking but with longer strides. The activity was smooth, fluid, and easy. I skied all day on narrow trails through the deciduous trees. Swales and mounds made the terrain interesting and required skill in sidestepping, edging and herringbone steps.

Cutting a new trail was like cutting through cotton candy, soft and light. The air was clear without an odor. In comparison to downhill, *this is the life! Pure cross-country freedom.* There were very few people in the woods. I came across perhaps 10 to 15 other skiers on the trails that day. What a contrast to downhill with crowded slopes with many noisy skiers packing the snow into hard icepack.

After a full day of non-stop movement, I returned home to find that I had lost five pounds. That's an easy diet plan!

The question of whether it is the equipment or the ability that matters surfaced again.

When I moved to Seattle in 1979, I naturally joined REI (Recreational Equipment, Inc.) and bought a pair of cross-country skis with real leather boots and sturdy toe clamp bindings. About eight years later, Joseph, my fiancé who had never cross-country skied decided to try the sport. He researched the pros and cons of equipment and bought a modern step-in pair that was supposed to be better than the old toe clamp binding. He believed that new technology would be superior to my older design. The new bindings that he selected were a step-in type and a lengthwise tongue and groove was supposed to keep the shoe on the ski. The ski itself was narrower than the old-fashioned skis.

We found that he could not break trail with the new flimsy design. Also, turning was difficult because the heel would slide sideways and off the ski. The newer skis were fine for straight, level, easy gliding. There would be no telemarking for him and no backcountry skiing. I was saddened that he did not enjoy cross-country skiing as much as I did. And he felt a little compromised that I had to break trail for him in powder.

He was right. Equipment does make a difference.

Wind Ensemble at Mount Baker *

Most people sleep at night. There is less activity outside and the quietness promotes resting. Rejuvenation occurs during sleep. I consider any nap time a form of meditation.

My sleeping habits were different in the city that never sleeps. In my early adolescence-probably until I was 11 years of age-my mother would tell me that I walked in my sleep. Typically, I would walk into my parent's bedroom, and she would get up and guide me back to bed. I believe that the door to my room was closed after a few of those excursions. On occasion, she would report my night's activities and a few times asked, "Why were you sleeping under your bed?" As if I had been awake to know. After finding me under the bed several times, she installed metal side rails to my bed's frame and that ended my excursion to some cave land I might have been dreaming about. One morning she said, "I opened the door to your bedroom to check on you and you sat up in bed and said, 'If that is the way you want it, that is the way you will get it'!" Those words were a common phrase of my mother's. "I thought that you were awake, but you laid right back down and were asleep."

My sleep was so heavy that those active excursions, wordy outbursts, and dreams were never remembered the following day. Little did I know that my adolescent wild nighttime antics would develop into beneficial skills needed in my older life.

In the '60s, I listened to acid rock. In the '70s and '80s, the hustle type dance music put me into a deep slumber. Waterbeds were popular in the 1970s and I had one. The movement fit my floating life-style. The realization of a dream. Free floating on water as the water conformed to my shape.

My boyfriend at the time bought a house and since I had spoken about the attributes of a waterbed, he bought one. No doubt with the intent of enticing me into marriage. Luther was about two and a quarter times my weight, I would be sleeping on a hill and he in a valley. How could I be comfortable?

I slept like a baby. In the morning I was surprised to not see him in bed. I trudged downstairs to find him in his bathrobe having coffee and making breakfast.

"How long have you been up?"

"Heck, Heather. I slept on the couch. You kicked, tossed and turned all night, rocking the bed. I couldn't get a moment's shut-eye."

At my small size, sleeping on a hill, how was that even possible?

Couples should sleep together. A marriage having separate sleeping arrangements would not last. We broke up shortly after that. I guess he loved the waterbed more.

I continued to enjoy listening to music and most likely exercised in my sleep throughout the night up until the mid-1980s. The music was quite soothing and drowned out vehicular, train, and conversations from the neighborhood.

Then I married Joseph.

We moved to a quiet neighborhood in Seattle and unlike me, Joseph has always had silence and no music after his bedtime at midnight. I was a bit resentful of not having music on; therefore our solution was to set a timer, around 10 p.m., for an hour or two of music as I drifted off to dreamland. Yet I still missed the all-night concerts.

At some point in our early marriage, Joseph said, "You kicked me square in the ass last night, pushing me to the edge of the bed."

"I did not!"

"Usually you run and flail only on your side of the bed, but last night you took over my side."

Yup, I think I missed the music. But also thankful that usually he could sleep through my nighttime antics.

In the '90s, I played the love songs of Yanny, and the passionate flamenco style of Segovia. During the 2000s, I rarely put music on and as a result I had trouble sleeping. I would wake at two o'clock in the morning and think, "Why sleep when I could be shopping?" Hardly anyone shops at that early hour and the whole ordeal took less than 20 minutes in the store. The whole escapade less than an hour. When I would arrive back home, my husband would still be snoring. He usually didn't know that I left the house. If I am super energized and have time, the baking pan comes out. Joseph wakes to aromas of hot coffee and freshly baked bread or cinnamon rolls.

But there wasn't always a nice scent of baked goods to wake up to. On occasion, Joseph would notice that I was not home after midnight. This was prior to cell phones, instant messaging and tracking devices.

"Where were you? I was frantic and couldn't figure out how someone might have broken in and kidnapped you."

"I couldn't sleep and didn't want to wake you. What else can I do at two in the morning?"

My sleeplessness and early morning outings began to happen more often.

"What are you doing? It is not so safe for you to be out alone and I don't know where you are. Are you having an affair?"

He knew of my father's philandering and thought that I might take after my dad in that regard.

To calm his notions, I agreed to not go out after midnight and found other activities to keep busy.

During the 2010s and 2020s, I used music again to help me sleep. I listened mostly to the songs of frogs, birds, and nature. The sounds of nature have always been a comfort at night. Joseph also enjoyed nature sounds and when we married he was relieved that he found someone who could sleep with him.

Gasp!

One of the reasons I no longer needed a radio or CD playing throughout the night, was that I have a ready orchestra in the room. Occasionally the sounds of a vibrating trombone, a drawn-out French horn, the whistle of a flute, or even snappy castanets will click out a melody. And ooohh, the crescendo might cause my legs to dance. While I sleep and rest, my eardrums most certainly get a workout.

Lest you not believe me...

In 1988, our friends, Dave and Diane who were members of the Mountaineers, invited us for a weekend of cross-country skiing on Mount Baker in the north Cascade region.

After an hour and a half drive, we arrived at the ski resort at about 9 a.m. The members of the Mountaineers had built a two-story wooden timber lodge in 1956. The lodge was built as an open-room concept. A large fireplace in the open living room and the large dining area provided ample area for socializing for a large group and several small groups. The kitchen was huge with a commercial-grade stainless sink and stainless counters. Upstairs the second floor had a vaulted ceiling, and open-timbered walls with perhaps one center structural wall. On both floors, the bathrooms were private and walled off.

After a full day of skiing, plus helping to prepare a community cooked and shared dinner and cleanup afterwards, we were worn out. There may have been about 25 of us to overnight in the lodge. Dead tired, we trudged upstairs to the sleeping accommodations. We knew that sleep would come quickly and pleasurable uninterrupted dreams would come in the silence of the night.

In those days, I was a heavy sleeper. I was accustomed to living in noisy neighborhoods. Friends would joke, "A bomb could go off and Heather would not hear it." This was partially true. No matter the volume, familiar noises would not stir me, but I did have survival instincts so any out-of-the-ordinary sounds would wake me.

We had our soft sleeping bags laid on wooden slatted beds. For middle-aged bodies, this was better than camping in a tent on rocky ground. Joseph and I were in an area near an exterior wall. Dave and Diane were a few bunks away closer to the mid-area of the building. Heavy timbers softened any sounds from the late-night stragglers downstairs and dampened any rustling sounds from their clothing and footsteps as they climbed the stairs. In the quiet stillness I fell asleep immediately.

Wait, what was that noise? I woke with eyes wide open and alert with a Swiss Army knife ready in my hand. It was very dark. I estimated the time to be about two in the morning. Joseph had played saxophone for years which may have contributed to his larger than normal lungs and windpipe. With the exhaustion and clean air, he was snoring much louder than usual. He made sounds like the low notes of a tenor horn with drawn-out fog horn blows. Yet that was not what woke me. There was some other exhalation. An exasperated sigh? I didn't move, but turned my head slightly and recognized Diane's outline. I could actually feel Diane glaring in our direction, huffing as she made her way downstairs. Did she not think that

Joseph's cacophony was music in the night? I do hope she got some rest, as the topic was not brought up the next day. Joseph was extremely loud. Might I estimate 70 decibels? As loud as a boisterous conversation or as soft as a classical trio. However your mind might perceive sound.

Joseph was not bothered by and did not hear Diane's exit. He did not stir. And I went right back to sleep listening to a wind ensemble.

* * *

Joseph isn't the only person with a large set of lungs taking the stage. I can contribute to bursts of wind turbulence and sounds of wind instruments also.

Explosion! A lot of black soot and dust was entering the office space. Black clouds being blown out from the HVAC ducts falling from the ceiling and landing on my desk. Another boom! A full force sneeze. That was the loudest sneeze ever emitted from her five foot two petit frame. What a set of lungs! Years ago a doctor reviewed my chest x-rays and commented that they were the longest set of lungs he had ever seen.

From the other side of the room, about 100 feet away, Harry came from his office, asking along the way, "Who was that?" No one wanted to say my name, yet heads and arms pointed toward my direction.

Five foot tall insulated cubicle dividers separated individual desks and workspaces. Tom sitting on the other side of a cubicle stood up and asked me, "Are you alright?"

My mother used to sneeze loudly. I believe her dramatics were done on purpose. Her "Eeeauuu!" at the end was a high pitched screech and lasted much longer than the actual sneeze. She was always dramatic and liked to be bigger than life. Later, long after I had moved out of the family home and was in my late 50s did I notice that her sneezes were much quieter. Normal. A regular ha-chew! And that was it.

Somewhere along the line of life, I developed an explosive sneeze. It happened sometime in my mid-thirties, after I moved to Seattle. Sometime after my hospital stay.

3 *The Working Life* *

"Do you want to know who you are? Don't ask. Act!
Action will delineate and define you." – Thomas
Jefferson, 3rd President of the United States

Over a 50-year time frame I have held 20 jobs. The shortest
employment of four hours was in a fast-food establishment.
The longest time spent under one employer lasted eleven and
a half years.

Not caring for schedules, typically I didn't set a goal, as I
changed residences or changed careers. Life simply took me.
I floated on energy and opportunities. The only sequence was
to ensure that I would be in a different or better situation than
before.

Path like a butterfly - I like to flit; and think, and talk
about the next best thing - what to do tomorrow, what to plan
for tomorrow. Life is so much more interesting when you can
adapt-find and work solutions for any issues. Had I stuck
to a schedule and been inflexible, I would not have taken
detours -like crew on Samarang and quit several jobs even
though I enjoyed the work and my co-workers. Most certainly
I would not have entertained living in another state than the
one I grew up in. I left many because I felt trapped. The feeling

of being trapped certainly causes a human to move, to devise ways of getting out.

The time spent working in offices were stints to simply keep the landlord happy having a paying renter; whereas outdoor work fulfilled my dream of adventure and diversity.

* * *

At seven years of age, I wanted to be like my dad. He was a Master Plumber. I wanted to be a Master Plumber. My child's view of the world was limited. When adults asked what I wanted to be when I grew up there were few vocations that I could name. The rhyme: "Rich man, Poor man, Beggar man, Thief, Tinker, Tailor, Indian Chief" gave me a head start to choose from, but none of these fairy tale vocations suited me. Stubborn, I stuck with the hopes of working as a plumber until I was about 12 years of age.

My fantasies only swirled as society dictated that females should be in kinder gentler vocations. But I wanted action. The word "No" was enunciated from my mother's lips often, whenever I asked for something that I really wanted. Like going to summer camp or learning to horseback ride. It seemed whenever I got what I wanted, the happening turned out wrong. She knew these things.

One of my good friends competed in horse shows and horseback jumping. I wanted to be like her and pestered my parents with questions and statements about doing the same. Finally, the day came when my mother took me for a private riding lesson at a small training center.

I was about 12 years old and didn't know a thing about horses, other than I wanted to ride a live one and perhaps really become a cowgirl. Carousels were for little kids. The jocks brought out two horses, and for some reason, they put me on the larger and very skittish horse. The horse snorted and stepped sideways away from me. One of the trainers held the reins tightly and helped to hoist me onto the horse as its back was above my head.

The leader rode ahead of me leading me through a level pasture and onto a narrow dirt trail in the trees which ran along the perimeter of the facility adjoining a busy road. My horse was stubborn and stopped to eat low-lying vegetation. The leader instructed, "Pull the reins up." My weak arms pulled, but this powerful horse took no notice. "Again, give a hard jerk." Still no notice. "Dig your heels into his side while pulling on the reins." Still no notice and no response. The heel pressure didn't work. "Give a hard swift kick!"

Although I was afraid to hurt the horse, patience was not my virtue. My powerful ice-skating legs gave one hard and swift kick. Within a second the horse's head shot up, the reins loosened, and he bolted into a gallop. This movement thrust me off of the saddle with my shoulder leading the way. Fortunately, I landed to the side away from his hoofs. The leader ran ahead to corral the runaway horse and brought him back to me. My shoulder hurt, but I felt okay even after the wind had been knocked out of me.

She hoisted me up onto the horse and I rode back to the stables with my shoulder throbbing with every trot. This must have been the second part of my inadequate lesson as the horses were actually trotting and not walking. What did I know.

I felt humiliated and sheepish about asking for things that I wanted and wondered if circumstances would always be like that.

My mother did not say much, but took me to a doctor to be checked out. After an x-ray, the doctor said, "You have a fractured shoulder. A cast is not needed, but you'll have to wear a sling for at least one week."

Mom asked about long-term use and complications.

"There will be less range of motion and the arm will be shorter than the other."

We would have to wait and see if the difference would affect my balance in ballet and in ice skating. I was not fully grown, but as genetics would dictate, I stopped growing fully that year without a noticeable difference in the length of my arms. I learned to write with my left hand for the many homework assignments that had to be completed that week. Not being able to lift my right arm nor move my hand without pain required multi-dexterity. What the doctor didn't mention was the probability of arthritis that would set in at an older age.

And that was sadly the end of my dream to become a cowgirl.

My First Office Job

Although I enjoyed working with my dad and wanted to help him in his real estate business, he discouraged me by not showing me the ropes. He was too busy. He tried to extol the benefits of having a government job. That way there would be time to work freelance on my main interests. Like he did.

My Dad was a workaholic. His motto was "Sleep is a waste of time. Why sleep, when I could be working and making money." He probably slept five hours at most every night, as he was working when I went to sleep and had already left for work when I woke at 6 a.m. The economic depression in the 1930s made his generation sensitive to poverty and he never wanted to be wanting again. To save a penny he would darn his own socks until there were more darning threads than the original sock material. He hardly bought anything new and was fairly inventive repairing items himself. He worked a full-time day job for the city's sewer department inspecting and repairing hydrants, sewer, and water lines. After evening dinners, he repaired commercial sewing machines in his tool shop area, which was in the same room as our basement kitchen. Our basement was divided into two rooms, plus a half bath. One open room held the washer/dryer, the kitchen along one wall, the oil furnace along the other wall, then his tool shop and a walk-in pantry. To save money, the thermostat was kept very low. I could never get warm at night. In the morning, the single pane windows would have frost on the inner panes during the coldest winters. The main room was our living area and his office.

He was also a licensed real estate broker along with an investing partner, Frank Palin. Not only did my father run the business, he also did most of the plumbing work in several of his apartment buildings, bought estate sale homes, refurbished them, and sold the houses at a profit.

For convenience and to save even more money, his real estate office was in our basement. In his spare time, that is where he would be. At his desk, making phone calls, recording rent receipts that he collected from his building superintendents, and paying bills into the late night. How he found time to be a husband, father and sugar daddy outside of the home, I can't imagine.

He loved wheeling and dealing. Years later when I applied for my real estate license, he excitedly advised me that, "Buying and selling real estate is like a love affair. A constant massaging. There is great anticipation in having your offer accepted, excitement in closing the deal, or heartbreak when deals fail."

That sounded like a roller coaster I wanted to ride.

He targeted homes that had been on the market due to estate sales and foreclosures. Many of the homes were in need of extensive repair. Being a Master Plumber he was able to repipe an entire home if needed. He also had experience from his four years in the Navy on steam tugs. All of the apartment buildings were heated by oil furnaces with steam radiators in each apartment, so he knew how to repair the heating systems. He sold the refurbished houses at huge profits.

Negative market perceptions, because someone had died in the house, were bonuses. Few buyers competed to purchase a property with a dark history. I remember two stories that he relayed regarding homes with spirits. He had just purchased and repainted an old two-story wooden house. As he climbed a ladder to change out an overhead dining room chandelier, the chandelier began to sway. This was New York, on bedrock. Not an earthquake prone area. The windows were closed, no wind and the furnace was turned off. He said that he was alone in the house and there was no air movement. Was the soul of the home trying to say something?

In another home, he was in the shower replacing the fixtures. Holding a wrench to undo the faucet, the wrench was suddenly knocked out of his hand and thrown to the ground two feet from the shower enclosure. There was no explanation.

There were other details and stories that I don't remember, but he was quite intuitive with houses and often felt a presence in rooms where someone had passed. I have inherited some of that intuitiveness.

Another motto my father used repeatedly to answer questions and comments about taking time to relax and taking a vacation or why not spend time with your daughter was "My work is my play." That motto was an early lesson on the importance of enjoying what one spends time on for one-third or more of a day. Later in life I realized that the play/work thought process is used by creatives. I never thought of him as being creative, but now I realize that he had a great imagination and fantasies. He had a fix or solution for many situations. When his tenants complained of being cold, he would check the thermostat, and pretend that he was adjusting something while his warm thick fingers covered the sensor. His explanation would be put forth something like this: "See, Mrs. Tenant, it's 74 degrees in here. Perhaps you need a sweater. The temperature is just right in here." When he was in the Navy, few of his fellow seamen were literate. He penned love letters to their female friends or wives that waited for them to return. Also, when at sea, he carved wooden boxes from salvaged wood. He amused himself, kept busy and enjoyed most days.

When it was time for me to start working a real job where I would have to pay income taxes, my father naturally advised to apply for a government job. The minimum age to apply for a federal job was 16. But I was only 15. That did not stop him from helping me to write a resume to apply for a file clerk position with the Social Security Administration in Queens.

Personnel called me to take the aptitude test, which consisted of about one hundred questions to be completed within a two-hour time frame. I remember that the majority of the questions covered basic math, identifying matched sets of numbers, editing, and proofreading. In grade school, I had scored high in spelling bees and was a fast reader. I found the test was simple for an entry-level position.

Out of about 25 or 30 applicants, I was the first to finish within an hour. The testing monitor cocked his head, narrowed his eyes, and looked at me in a strange questioning way, as I handed in the test.

At some point, I was called for an interview. The interviewer could not believe that I scored so high at 98 percent and well within the two-hour time allowed. He asked if I had taken the test before. No doubt, I would start my first office job within the month at a salary somewhere below 490 dollars per month.

Of course, at that age, my real age of 15, I did not have a driver's license. Fortunately, the office was within a ten-minute walk of my home. In the late 1960s, the neighborhood was still safe for a young woman to walk alone. Never one to dawdle or waste time, I clocked my speed at five miles per hour and each day strode through two blocks of single-family homes, hurried past a block of uninteresting brick apartment buildings, which led to a few blocks of small businesses. I took in the passing smells of bakeries, delicatessens, and pizza parlors. Focused on getting to work, I never stopped moving until I reached a traffic signal at Queens Boulevard, a retail and commercial area of larger buildings housing department stores, and office buildings. It was hard to bypass my favorite department store, Alexanders. Alexanders was the store to shop at for the up and coming working person. Racks were jam packed with clothing and all styles were in every color, and size.

Across the boulevard and a block or two more sat the Social Security building. Beyond that was LeFrak City. A low to middle-income housing project that was developed by Samuel

J. LeFrak, who was the father-in-law of Geraldo Rivera, the television reporter.

The Social Security building contained file cabinet after file cabinet. Rows of file cabinets filled with thousands of individual social security recipient records. I believe there may have been about 20 file clerks. There were two rows of tables and we sat two to a table. We would receive correspondence, retrieve the associated file, and refile the folders. All boring day long.

In many ways I took after my dad working or playing on numerous projects throughout the day and night. From age 15 to 17, while working full time in the day, I attended Bryant Evening High School and obtained a General Education Diploma.

After three years of mind-numbing duties at Social Security, I left to enter York College to continue my education during the day. That lasted one semester. The college was a few miles away from my apartment in Woodhaven. Subways are fine transportation if you are wearing combat gear and have protection. Running shoes, muscular legs, mace and a four-inch blade were my instruments of defense. I felt unsafe on this route of the subway, and as I ran through the neighborhood of Jamaica.

* * *

In my 20s, my best friend Diane and I were going through a time of discovery of who we were or rather the dream of what we wanted to be and who we wanted to be. It was also a time of body styling. Dressing and looking to impress and to be seen, we shopped the latest fashions and partied late into the nights. We considered changing our names. Names such as Morgan, Rockefeller, Britney, and Mercedes were seriously tossed around.

Our names didn't change, but our styles and vocations did. Diane had studied political science in college, yet she pursued clothing design. I was studying to be a legal secretary. But I failed stenography and had no back-up plan and no long-term goals.

Again, I needed a job to pay my rent. I submitted several resumes for daytime file clerk positions. My college records were transferred to Baruch College, in Manhattan, which I would attend at night.

My First Real Job

It was 1974 and I had recently seen the movie *"The Towering Inferno"* starring my heroes Paul Newman and Steve McQueen. The movie won an Academy Award for Best Picture, which didn't surprise me, as I found the movie to be intense yet believable. A 138-story building in flames. I would not want to be in that situation or even be a witness to such a catastrophe, yet the action was riveting on the movie screen.

Shortly after seeing this movie, I was called for a job interview with one of the top 10 accounting firms in the world. Peat, Marwick, Mitchell and Company, what a coup! The offices were located right in the elite heart of Manhattan, on Park Avenue. A sophisticated difference from the middle-class neighborhood in Queens where I lived in a simple basement studio apartment in a 1930s single-family home.

On the day of the interview, I exited the subway station and headed towards 345 Park Avenue. The building was known as the Bristol-Myers Squibb building and PMM & Co. occupied most of the floors. At 44 floors it was one of the taller edifices in the area and quite modern having been built only four years prior. It was a beautiful sunny day and my euphoria blanketed car noises from traffic, car horns and other distractions from pedestrians as interview questions and answers occupied my mind. At a quick pace I walked along Park Avenue with my eyes riveted on the towering building as the full skyscraper came into view.

Oh dear; could that be orange flames at the upper floors of the building? Scenes from the movie came into my mind. Oouu, should I turn around? Apprehension set in as I slowed my walking pace. I thought, "This could be my first real job and with a prestigious company. Don't stop now, do not turn around. Don't make an emergency where there isn't one. There are no flames; the blaze is simply the sun reflecting off the windows projecting an orange glow." Pushing myself along I picked up my walking pace, headed towards the lobby and entered the elevator to the 38th floor with my heart in my throat.

The halls and offices were well decorated. The employees were hard at work, comfortably isolated each in their individual small room. Fine artwork hung on the walls and sculptures stood on pedestals. Certainly more expensive, posh, elegant, and expansive than my humble, undecorated, two windowed, studio apartment. The surroundings and the reputation of the firm overcame any apprehension that I might have had. I had to work here.

So, yes, the interview went well. I looked forward to living eight hours a day in posh surroundings. Visions of fires and emergency exits were still in my mind. Thankfully, the file room was located in the basement, without windows to the outside and only one flight of stairs to an outdoor exit. One full wall of the room was windowed that looked out to the stenographer pool of perhaps 20 women typing all day. I preferred moving around and filing, yet for an unknown reason, I was asked by the supervisor of the steno pool to proofread their finished products. The supervisor was perhaps in her mid-thirties and had been on the job for a number of years. She was a fast reader and we would take turns reading our copy out loud while the other person would mark up her copy. This was a thrill for me as we were both quick and on each read, I tried to read or proof faster than on the previous.

Later I was promoted to Benefits Clerk inputting new employee health and insurance elections. And again, promoted to an analytical position to calculate benefits.

All of these positions were located in a secure basement. Although I was confined to a desk all day, I never tired of working there. Variety makes a work day more interesting and on occasion I had great satisfaction by filling in as Executive Secretary on the 44th floor. I felt important, grown up and professional, representing and being the front face of the company for clients and traveling employees.

Throughout my four years of employment with PMM & Co., no emergencies occurred. Not even one fire drill.

* * *

Manhattan was the most appropriate borough in which to live and I had hoped to live there near my new job on desirable Park Avenue. However, I could not afford to live in that high rent district. Rather than walk, which was my preferred mode of transportation, I relied on the noisy subway as the fastest way into Manhattan. The route was fairly safe and most commuters were professional, well-dressed passengers. Many train cars were not air-conditioned. The 90 plus degree summer heat restricted the amount of combat gear that I could wear. I am thankful though that I never had to use my knife. My shoes were another weapon.

One winter, dressed in office attire, high heels, stockings, dress and a long heavy coat I managed to squeeze into a subway car by breathing in and tightening my muscles. We stood shoulder to shoulder, hip to hip with strangers pretending that they weren't there. Soon I felt some pressure in an area where there should not have been pressure. I looked down to see a man's hand pressed up against my breast. Viewing his arm up to his pale face with gibbous eyes was a mid-thirties balding masher. I don't know what he was getting out of this, but I was glad that I had a heavy coat on. The train was screeching to a halt at my stop. I turned my back towards him to face the doors, lifted my powerful leg, and gave one strong flamenco style stomp with my steel stiletto heel on the top arch of his foot. He stayed in the car with a grimace on his face.

The first portion of my commute was in a safer Queens borough by bus. Thus sandwiched between passengers while holding the overhead leather straps, I was able to take naps.

With a solid paying job, I looked to improve my living situation. There was an ad in the newspaper for a basement apartment in my old neighborhood. I grabbed the vacancy and spent a year there until the owners kicked me out.

Because the house was a single family, I did not want to disturb the owners living above me. I never had any parties and spent most evenings and weekends out. One day after work there was an unexpected knock on the door. "What have you been doing here? The police came, searched the apartment and were asking about your friends. What do you know about this? We can't have this type of behavior here, and the neighbors thinking that we are renting to a criminal! We want you out by the end of the month!" The owners did not wait for an answer.

Even though I was not directly involved in criminal activity, apparently the suspicion that my friends were was enough.

I then spent about a year in a cockroach infested studio apartment on Grand Avenue in the neighborhood of Woodside. After moving in, I spent the second evening pouring boric acid into every crevice in the closets and door joints, and pushing steel wool into any crack that was large enough. That helped to reduce the number of roaches. The brick building, half a block from the elevated train, actually rattled when the train passed. The majority of brick apartment buildings built in Queens were stark inside, but built to last centuries with stone tiled floors and staircases built with marble steps.

It was here that I realized how much others spy on and watch others.

I had my work and play routine. This encompassed working five days a week from Monday through Friday, and either partying or attending college classes at night. I had saved enough money to take a short four-day vacation. I secured the apartment and to not be conspicuous I carried a small overnight bag. That seemed to be enough of a diversion from my routine for someone to notice that the apartment was vacant. When I returned, the door was ajar. Luckily, the second security lock held and the criminals were not able to gain entry and no damage was done to the door. Living alone, I took extra precautions each time I left the apartment and kept the extra security lock on the door engaged and the window closed. Access from the metal fire escape might be too tempting for some.

By the mid-70s I could see my neighborhood beginning to break down. Property owners seemed to take less interest in maintaining their homes. Crime was on the rise. My commutes were becoming a run for your life course. From home, a five-minute run to the subway to endure a compressed standing room only, unairconditioned subway car. Commuters stood close enough to iron out your clothing. Then a fast walk to the office in Manhattan in order to arrive there safely.

At this point, I started to have occasional nightmares. I dreamt of Manhattan (The City) being bombed, fires, riots, and other catastrophes. These dreams were unnerving and eventually occurred so frequently that I decided it was time to leave New York.

The world was an open destination.

The Search

The first invitation to visit and relocate was from a grade school friend who had moved to Chicago with her husband. We had been close friends throughout high school and college and kept in constant contact by phone and mail since her move a year prior. We missed seeing each other. "Heather, please come out and visit. Bob and I are located near the downtown area; there is so much to do here. Bob can recommend you for a position in his company." The visit and opportunity to move there was a great temptation. Being near the Great Lakes was intriguing to me as I would be near the water to enjoy boating. My weekend visit over a Thanksgiving weekend provided sufficient opportunity for an overview of what it would be like to live in the city. Chicago, although smaller than New York, was too much like New York except for the brisker frigid winds that blow off Lake Michigan. Winds are not my favorite component of weather and the wind blew me out of there. Even the slow snowy crawl to the airport did not delay me long enough to stay.

I reconnected with friends in Germany. For the tours, I packed clothing that was similar in their style so I wouldn't appear to be a tourist and I ate German food. Eventually I would smell like the locals and blend in. We visited many beer halls!

The point is, I was ready to immerse myself in their culture by speaking, looking, acting, eating, and smelling like the locals.

I revisited Frankfurt, Germany. Another grade school friend had forsaken New York and moved back to her hometown. Carrie worked in a bank and could provide good references for me to obtain work. From previous travels, I also knew another family nearby in Frankfurt am Main and another good friend lived in the Olympic Village complex in Munich. Having those contacts and a passable knowledge of the German language, the transition would have been easy to make. However, in the late 1970s, I found their cultural attitudes did not make it easy. Germans were stodgy. The younger generation had not come into their own as yet. Different rules applied to male-female manners and relationships. Women who smoked were looked at in distaste. Pay scales were lower for women than for men. Women were expected to marry and have children. I left disappointed, but glad that those aspects of their culture were theirs to uphold.

I was not there to change them and I could and would adapt to the culture of the place where I would move to. After all, I was looking to be in a better place.

I spent many vacations with friends and relatives in Florida, Virginia, and Puerto Rico and visited other countries as well, always reviewing the lifestyles and livability for a possible permanent relocation.

After two years of searching and reading newspapers from large cities in other states, I was beginning to become frustrated and desperate. The nightmares were becoming more intense and my desire to leave New York was overpowering.

After narrowing my options to three or four cities, I was unable to decide. I asked my dear, newly relocated to Seattle from New York, friends (who had previously scoffed at my intention of leaving the best city in the world) the crucial question, "Tell me the truth, does it really rain that much in Seattle?"

To which they answered "Oh no! The rain is only a light drizzle." So, to be thorough and continue my research, I compared annual rainfall statistics and saw that Seattle's total precipitation was less per year than in New York. I can handle a little drizzle.

On 10 out of 13 moves or places where I have lived, I have little to no recollection how the moves were made. In New York I did not have a car nor a driver's license until I was 23 years of age. I owned a suitcase and hangars. Moves were easy when sharing furnished apartments. But for the apartments which I furnished, who moved me, where or how I bought beds and couches, are lost memories.

I do remember the move from New York to Seattle. I packed a few belongings into two bulging suitcases with bare necessities, boarded an airplane, and exuberantly left New York in August of 1979. After a couple of months, my mother shipped my father's WWII Navy wooden trunk loaded with kitchen supplies.

At that time of year, the Seattle core was beautiful and warm. The air was clean and Mount Rainier stood out against clear blue skies. On sunny days the mountain was always visible from Capitol Hill and Queen Anne Hill.

The sucker hole did not prepare me for the wet winter weather. That light everyday drizzle was a misery to me, yet I decided to stick it out. Luckily, a little snow saved the dreariness of that winter.

As the following winter approached, I knew I had to overcome my distaste for dreary, saturated days. How would I do this? Various scenarios floated through my mind. Move to San Francisco, California where a friend from New York had relocated to or perhaps anywhere in sunny California? Hole up and read books by the fire? Luckily, I had met quite a few boaters. We sailed all winter and in all stormy weather. And I loved boating. Gale force winds stopped the ferries, but harsh weather did not stop us. That was the cure. Thereafter, the occasional little drops of drizzle no longer daunted me.

Seattle proved to be a wonderful place for discovery.

I decided to stay.

With that relocation, my adventures were about to begin......

The Saving of a Move

For the first month, I stayed with my relocated friends, Diane and Nick, in their apartment on Capitol Hill, Seattle. Capitol Hill has many flat roofed, brick apartment buildings. The neighborhood reminded me of the areas and buildings that I lived in in Woodhaven and Jamaica, in Queens, New York. This made me feel more at home. A lovely large studio apartment in one of those brick buildings became vacant and available. My apartment faced south with windows looking into another apartment building, but if I looked sideways and stuck my head out of the window, looking past a not-so-coveted view of Interstate 5, a coveted view of snow-covered Olympic Mountains to the west was captivating on a clear day. I loved this apartment, aside from the apartment manager who would let himself in without knocking or ringing the doorbell to deliver mail packages. He was a nice man and harmless, just a bit quirky. The apartment was perfect for me, partly furnished with a Murphy bed and built-in settee in the kitchen. The stove was all-electric, which took some adjustment to get used to as I burned a few meals. The electric heating element was either on or it was off. Cooking with gas is more flexible. You can fine-tune the heat and the distance from the flame. Enabling more control over speed and timing.

I would have stayed here if it weren't for a man. He thought the apartment was too small for two. What? I like cozy.

He didn't have a job so it was fortuitous that we found a two-bedroom large apartment in another flat-roofed, brick building where he would be the building manager. In exchange for a few hours of work each week, collecting rents, changing light bulbs, showing apartments to prospective tenants, and cleaning out vacated units, our spacious unit was rent free.

After a year or so, the job did not work out and we moved to a more modern 1960s flat-roofed, brick building with a central courtyard surrounding a cool water swimming pool. That was lovely. Usually, we were the only swimmers and we used the pool even on cold nights.

The apartment was within a ten-minute walk to my job at Pemco Insurance. This was an office job and it paid the rent. I worked the swing shift from late afternoon to midnight. Perfect timing freed my days for sailing.

* * *

KOMO-TV STAFF news update – 10 p.m. PDT Saturday, August 29, 2009. 'Two men arrested Friday night during a bizarre shooting spree along Interstate 5 in North Seattle may have been planning to fire at vehicles driving up and down the freeway...

This news story brought my thoughts back to the well-documented time span of the I-5 Bandit. The span, of which his known crimes occurred, was between October 9, 1980 and February 15, 1981. Also known as The I-5 Killer he was apprehended on March 7, 1981.

During that timeframe, I was working at Pemco Insurance Company in Seattle. Our open-spaced office was located on the third floor. Desks were adjoined and situated close to the exterior walls of the building. Large windows faced east in line with Interstate 5. Not a great view, but it allowed a lot of light in during the day. During the evening, the vertical blinds were left open for a reflected view of the office.

I was one of six Small Claims Representatives working the 4 p.m. to midnight shift. The rest of the building was unoccupied.

Around 10 p.m. it was pitch black outside and quiet. Inside, bright fluorescent lighting lit our paperwork. The usual sounds of voices on phone calls with claimants and paper shuffling tended to diminish as the shift wore on.

Ping, bang, crack! Wide eyed and motionless, ready to fall to the floor in seconds, I saw a good-sized crack and a couple of etched circles in the windows. It was apparent that shots had been fired at us from a passing vehicle. Fortunately, the bullets did not penetrate the thick glass.

We never learned the identity of the shooter. After the incident, window shades were drawn for safety.

As a claims representative for vehicle and property damages, I became more aware that unintentional accidents can occur at any time. It is best to be on your guard and prepared for emergencies.

4 An Unexpected Detour

Weighting

The 1980s was an era of body awareness. That was nothing new for me as I had always been geared toward athleticism. Walking, tennis, ice-skating, and skiing were constant companions. In my late 20s I had an added interest in body sculpting. The routine encompassed a warm-up 15 minute fast walk to the gym, which was located a half mile from my apartment. I would first change into athletic gear, then jog for 10, weight circuit for 30, and swim for 30. At seven o'clock in the morning I had the pool to myself. Floating on the placid surface the repetitive movement of my arms and legs removed the clutter and chaos from my mind. The laps were meditative, my mind was quiet, but on occasion when there was a problem to solve, answers to questions often came to me and showcased in my mind as the soft swishing of water streamed past my ears. Following this workout, a meditative time in the sauna and steam bath relaxed and lengthened my muscles. This routine ended with a hot shower followed by a cold shower to energize all systems. I believed that I could handle anything after that.

Aside from this twice a week routine, sporting activities continued as well. My body felt very alive and very much in control. I could feel and isolate any part of my body at any given moment by twitching a muscle. Every cell in my body was activated and working at their peak. Total body orgasms were at a sensual height. My lovers touch on my toe would send sensations up my leg, thigh, and beyond.

My oxygen levels were high and my brain and thought processes were perfectly clear. I had never felt better in my life and wanted to feel these results forever. The workouts were at times boring and tedious but the payoff was well worth the time spent. I was able to be independent, carry my own luggage. Basically, take care of things by myself.

Motorcycles were a passion at that time too. Two wheels were the only way to commute. Light and free. If everyone had a motorcycle, the road would be full of considerate drivers. There would be fewer accidents and less air pollution. But unfortunately, most people purchase an easy sedan ride.

There were days when moments of blurry, illusion-quick flashes of a car crossing in front of me would occur. A guardian angel trying to warn me. The flashes would come as I drove my car on Interstate 5. A quick blur on the side, a dark sweep of lights and movement of a vehicle, a slight whoosh. Was the blur coming from the left or the right? I couldn't tell. It was so fast. I tried to negate these visions by closing my eyes and shaking my head. I did not want to believe it. At 27 years of age, I was still indestructible and an alert driver. Nothing would happen. These flashes were overridden by a feel-good positive attitude of immortality. If you think bad thoughts, they will happen. Right? Fool, why did I not listen to these warning flashes?[2]

DÉJÀ VU – The Ride of a Lifetime

"Hello, this is Little Leaf's Bookstore. Your book order is ready for pick-up. We will hold it for you whenever you are ready."

I had been anxiously waiting for that call for over a week. That phone call changed the course of my life. Not because it resulted in reading the book, it was the journey.

Every year, during Thanksgiving week, I would fly to Florida to visit my father, and in 1982 my plan was no different. I would pack a small carry-on and fly out on either Delta or American. He lived in a sprawling town near the Gulf. Not having much to do while visiting a suburban area, I spent the majority of my time reading and exercising. My father, although 'retired', was actively running his plumbing business and was gone every day. I had ordered a new book to read expecting delivery a few days before my departure. That phone call came at the very last day possible to have time to pick it up prior to my week-long vacation.

At the time, I lived in Seattle but most of my weekends were spent with friends in Kingston. It made sense to order a book from their local neighborhood bookstore. But now it was inconvenient that the bookstore was located eight miles

---

[2] If time is linear, we would only remember the past and not see or have glimpses of the future. Time must be circular – 24 hours, days, years, earth revolving and so distant time (the future) has circled before us.
'for the things that are seen are transient, but the things that are unseen are eternal.' 2 Corinthians 4:18

north of the Winslow ferry terminal on Bainbridge Island. I estimated that if I left Seattle by two o'clock, I could be at the bookstore before closing. The ride would be smooth, as the weather was clear and crisp. Not one to waste time, I jumped on my motorcycle, a Honda 250 cc, and headed for the Seattle to Bainbridge ferry.

There is a sense of wild freedom and control in riding. The purring smooth sound of the engine puts me into a meditative, open monitoring Zen-like observation zone. Even so, every fiber in my body is on full alert. Accelerating through each gear brings an exhilarating rush as you hear the engine moving through the gears. K-vroom, K-vroom. Feelings of being one with the machine, each movement of your body controls the movement of the motorcycle and likewise, each turn or bump the bike makes transfers to your body and you react. I was in tune with the interactive drive.

I rode in all sorts of weather. Body fitting leather jacket and medium blue leather pants with ankle to calf zippers protected me from the elements. Even a pool of rainwater that would collect between my legs in the rainy Pacific Northwest did not deter me. Different driving techniques were used depending on the surface of the road. For example, one never drove a straight line on a grated bridge. Fun. Fun. Fun.

Bainbridge Island was rural in the early 1980s. Fewer than 3,000 inhabitants lived within 916 square miles. By early evening I was in Winslow and had just picked up my book at the strip mall shopping center and was heading back on a two-lane road, and on schedule to make the Winslow ferry run at 6 p.m. The lane widened adding a right turn to the main highway. As I passed the vehicle ahead of me to take the right lane, I saw the right front lights of a vehicle that had turned left from the opposite direction. I didn't see the flash; there wasn't a minute flash warning. I immediately applied the clutch and brake. The flash from my visions was happening. Although reality was different, it happened almost as fast and was confusing. There was no time to know if that action slowed me down, but their vehicle kept on going. The impact hit my front tire and hurled my body into the air. What seemed like a second in time, my waist landed on the car's front fender and knocked the breath out of me. Whoosh. I could not breathe.

My left hip hit the ground. I had no air to breathe and I was in no condition to attempt to regain my breath. I felt like a rag doll that was thrown down. I thought about traffic, "My Lord, this is might be the end. I'll be run over." I was unable to adjust my movement to get out of the roadway. In a few seconds, I was inert and internally bruised. Somehow my breath returned and I opened my eyes. I looked up, or rather to the side. It seemed like the road was not there. Someone's sturdy hands were on my shoulders trying to turn me around.

"Don't turn me." I must have whispered as a man tried to turn me onto my back. I heard some muffled voices and sensed that they were increasing in volume. As I was lying on my side, the man's hands moved to take my helmet off. My hands went up immediately to prevent him from removing my helmet. Instinctively I knew that if there was a problem with my neck, he could make my situation worse.

But what was my situation? I remembered a bump to the front tire and then someone trying to turn me on the ground. I can only imagine my flight through the air then hitting the fender of a car with my waist. I felt nothing and saw nothing.

I asked the man who was holding my helmet, "Have the police been called?"

Another man standing behind him said, "I am a medic and the police are on their way."

Already? That was fast. I must have blacked out. A fire station ambulance arrived with more medics. I had removed my eyeglasses and cried as I told the medic that I felt sick and nauseated. "Can you walk?" he asked.

They helped me to stand up and guided me as I limped, bent over, and in pain to the stretcher. In the ambulance, the medics checked my eyes and blood pressure. "It hurts here on my left side." I showed them the area. They poked my left side and squeezed my ribs, adding to my pain.

At the fire station, I was able to walk into the building and paced the room. I was in distress, not only because of the accident, but I also wondered if I would miss the eight o'clock ferry. If so, the next ferry was an hour later and was the last run of the evening. If I could be on that ferry, I could still get a good night's sleep and be refreshed for the flight to Florida in the morning. My father and step-mother were expecting to meet me at the Tampa airport. I did not want to disappoint them.

I continued pacing while worrying about my motorcycle and whether there was any damage. The medics were watching me closely. "Don't worry. Your motorcycle was taken to Anderson's Repair. There was minimal damage to the fender," one of the firemen told me. I sighed with relief. That was one less problem to worry about.

"Is there someone who can drive you to the ferry?" a medic asked.

They offered the fire station's phone to me. A friend who lived in Kingston didn't answer his phone. I knew no one else's phone number on the island.

I was beginning to feel a bit flushed and weak as we sat on a couch and the medics continued to observe me. "How will I know if I am okay or have internal bleeding?" I asked as I continued crying.

"You will have some dizziness; urine will be bloody and you will be weak."

The medics were talking amongst themselves, but I was not conscious of what they were saying as I was deep in my own thoughts.

The aches and pains throughout my torso limited my ability to walk upright, but I was not dizzy and I didn't have to go to the bathroom. They did not treat me for shock and they determined that I was well enough to take the ferry. One of the younger medics drove me to the ferry. He seemed concerned and caring. "If you still don't feel well, you can see a doctor at the Winslow Clinic."

I got onto the 7:30 p.m. ferry and by this time had to go to the ladies' room. I was walking slower than before, along with a limp. Sitting on the toilet, my urine felt abnormally warm and as I looked down all I saw was blood spurting out which filled the toilet.

At that point, I realized I might be in shock. *Am I in shock?* Past first aid courses didn't help me to understand what was happening. I only knew that I needed to stay calm. The half-hour ferry ride would be an impossible transit for me alone and I rushed to get off of the ferry before the horn blew to set sail. *Will they helicopter me over to Harborview?* On shaky legs I walked off the ferry to the ticket booth to get help. Steadying myself with my hands on the ticket booth I asked the ticket clerk to call an ambulance. At this point, the blue blood vessels that usually stood out on the top of my hands were no longer visible. Because I was able to stand and speak, the ticket clerk was hesitant to call for an ambulance. After several questions, he picked up the phone.

The medics returned and took my vitals. *Did I appear okay?* He must have noticed that I was in a daze with labored shallow breathing, because he called the emergency Winslow Clinic for the on-call doctor. His voice sounded like he had to do a lot of convincing that a doctor should come out after hours and see me immediately. I walked to the ambulance and sat on the front seat. I felt like death and then laid down. Medics continued to monitor my vital signs on the way to the clinic. Finally, the local on-call doctor arrived. After examining me, she realized that indeed this had been a serious accident. She took a blood sample and put in an IV. There was nothing else that she could do, except to call for an emergency ferry. No emergency ferry was available. The next scheduled run was at 8:50 p.m. Winslow did not have facilities to care for accident patients. She had decided that the best course of action was to have me transported to the trauma center in Seattle. Harborview Hospital would be at minimum an hour and a half away. The question I feared to ask was, with an open interior wound and loss of blood, would I last that time frame? She called the Bainbridge ambulance to transport me.

Finally, the ambulance arrived. The volunteer driver staggered out of the vehicle. He was several feet away yet his breath wafted towards me and reeked of alcohol. The island was not heavily populated and the majority of the fire fighters and medics were volunteers. There isn't a lot of choice when an on-call volunteer is having a great time at a party and an unexpected life or death call is received.

Meanwhile, I was still lying on the stretcher and he opened the ambulance door as the stretcher began to roll down the sloped parking lot. It was a blessing that I was still coherent. "Hey! I am rolling!" I yelled in time for him to sprint and hold the stretcher. Somehow, he managed to move me into the ambulance without any further mishaps.

I still suffered some lower-level pain throughout my body, which was amplified by every little movement of the ambulance. Navigating over rough bumps and driving onto the ferry increased the constant throbbing pain in my side and stomach. The thirty-minute ferry ride was smooth, but getting from the Seattle ferry terminal to Harborview, only a mile away, seemed like an interminable amount of time on a wash-board.

A good friend of mine had been a medic in New York City. He had told me stories of driving on streets jammed with traffic, trying to weave and straddle lanes when cars don't move over. Delays caused too many casualties.

I wanted to tell the drunken driver to speed up, but I reconsidered saying anything. A faster speed would amplify the jarring motion of the ambulance. What if he were to get into an accident along the way? The siren alone increased my apprehension without having to worry about another collision.

About 9:30 p.m., I was finally admitted to Harborview. I kept my eyes open to monitor every movement of the medic. In taking me out of the ambulance, the driver failed to unhook the IV bag from the wall nearly tearing the needle out of my arm. Thankfully, I was awake and cognizant enough to remind him to unhook it.

Having been raised by an unsympathetic mother who had worked for many years as a Registered Nurse in emergency and as a surgical assistant, she had taught me to be wary of doctors and nurses. She knew of too many errors in judgment [1] which resulted in mishaps and she was against excessive treatments, general and local anesthesia, and elective surgery. I was not knowledgeable about these procedures. How would I know if the doctors were doing the right thing? As long as I was awake, I had to keep my wits about me. I relinquished myself but then I really had no choice. I felt lost. What could I do? I had no real life experience in trauma care nor surgery and could offer no advice or stop them if they made a mistake.

My stomach felt overly warm and with every bump and jolt while being wheeled into the emergency room resulted in a little extra pressure of pain.

During my exercise regimes, I enjoyed feeling and being aware of every nerve in my body. But here, I preferred not to be in tune with my body. I wished to be out of my body and not feel anything.

They took a few x-rays, then another IV was inserted, also a catheter. The doctors were trying to determine where the bleeding was coming from by palpating my torso. The doctor said, "I am going to insert this tube into your nose. Swallow it down."

Not delicately, she began to insert a tube into my nostril with the end of the tube scratching my nose and back of my mouth. I tried to swallow, hating the sharp prong. Waving my hand at her to not continue, I pleaded, "I can't stand anything in my nose."

The frustrated ER doctor in a loud firm voice said, "Swallow this, or I will shove it down your throat!"

Oh shit. Quite surprised I swallowed fast.

A local anesthetic may have been shot into my waist, I do not recall because I felt nothing as they sliced a two-inch incision at my waist.

I was curious to watch what they were doing and wondered what the opening looked like. Then I had second thoughts. *If I am in shock, how would I react to seeing a big hole in my waist? Maybe I better not look. Just relax and let the doctors do what they know how to do.* My fate was in their hands.

* * *

Although there were no broken bones, a few more x-rays were taken. The doctors were still trying to discover the source of the bleeding. The excessive x-rays were questionable, since x-rays won't show soft tissue clearly, if at all. They had me sign an authorization form to conduct certain procedures including an arteriogram, and asked if there was anyone I needed to contact. At this point, I realized that I would not be visiting my father for the weekend. I shared a house with two of my best friends and I gave them that phone number. They dialed the phone and luckily, my friend Nick was home. I told him the situation and asked him to call my dad to say I would not be able to come, but that I would be okay. They did not have to come to Seattle.

There were two doctors working on me and perhaps an assistant somewhere in the room. A catheter was inserted to pump the blood out of my torso. Then an iodine dye was injected into my veins to reveal the area where the blood was seeping from. They instructed me to lie still and not to move a muscle while they took a picture, as the liquid would feel a bit warm.

Beware when doctors tell you it will hurt just a little, or be a bit uncomfortable.

When they snapped the picture, I screamed at the top of my lungs, "I am burning up!" and jerked a little, as all of my muscles tightly contracted. They quickly held my ankles down. My whole body felt like it was on fire. The pain concentrated on my lower back and right inner thigh. If I moved too much, another picture would have to be taken. Gripping the edge of the stretcher, I exhaled deeply and focused on curling my toes tightly to teleport the pain to a smaller area. That did not help much. I refocused trying to relax and think of being somewhere else, like a sandy beach with calm blue skies. That soothed me a little. The picture must have been clear enough, because another was not needed. After that, they inserted an additional IV and wheeled me into intensive care. The hot dye had by then cooled, but caused an ache throughout my whole body.

A nurse came and administered three units of blood. "Please, I am very thirsty. I need water."

"Sorry, but you are not allowed any liquids, not even ice."

My throat was so dry, I tried to swallow mucous to wet my throat, but there was none.

Lying there, I was too sore to move. Any slight move was more than uncomfortable. However, my eyes turned seeking feedback and information. Boring ceiling, bright lights. There were lots of voices and machines beeping. Is the nurse checking on me? I could not turn my head enough to see anything other than the ceiling. I could hear motion, and visualize the surroundings, but no one was nearby.

The lights are so bright, I will close my eyes. It must be about midnight. I am so tired; dare I go to sleep? It is so dark with my eyes closed. When people die, they say a bright light is seen. I don't see a light. It is so dark. Is that bad? Does the darkness mean I am not going to die or something else?

I hear a man's voice behind me. From the sound waves of his voice, I can tell he is sitting up. He has an accent and is talking non-stop, joking and chuckling. I think to myself; Isn't this an ICU? If he is so alert, what is he doing here? His voice is making me tired; he is annoying. I want to shout *Shut-up*, but I am too tired.

I don't know how long I was in intensive care, or if I even slept, but the next day I was still on the gurney, being wheeled onto an elevator. This was no smooth ride. Hospital floors may be fairly clean and smooth, yet the little bits of sand that the wheels rolled over jarred me, and at every slow turn I could feel increased pressure on my side as the force angled my body ever so slightly. The little jolt as the gurney wheeled over the space between the floor and the elevator felt like I was being thrown back down on the ground.

Three days into my confinement, my best friends, and roommates, Nick and Diane, came to visit. I was not much of a conversationalist as I dozed in and out of sleep. They left shortly afterwards.

Doctors came and went. They always probed my still sore torso. At last, some relief to have the tube that was down my nostril finally removed.

Harborview Hospital is a public facility and also a teaching hospital. Closely affiliated with the University of Washington, students and interns take rounds under the lead of an experienced doctor. The stomach probing was becoming tedious. Especially when four or five interns were watching and taking their turns practicing their examination procedures. I looked at them. I took my mind elsewhere, to a real bed-fantasizing what I could do with them. The fellows were so good-looking. I pictured what their muscular bodies looked like under their white coats. At least my hormones were working. Yet, there I was, in a hospital bed, in an immobile condition and not able to do anything.

On the fourth day, I was relieved to have one of the IV's removed and also the catheter. Nurses helped to turn me in bed every few hours and to get up. My temperature was up and now there was a urinary tract infection to deal with.

The next day, my fever was still high. The nurses tried to bring it down with two alcohol baths and three ice packs without success. In the morning, a Tylenol suppository seemed to help.

The nurses were urging me to walk around the floor to get some exercise. I was able to walk slowly for about five minutes at a time in the morning and once in the evening. Each day, walking a bit more.

On the fifth day, Emil, my supervisor, came to visit. Always trying to be a good host, I tried to engage in conversation and be presentable by being out of bed. This was quite trying. I felt fairly well before he came, but after a half hour of sitting up and talking, I was exhausted and had a relapse which lasted about four hours and I felt worse than the day before. Again, I wouldn't and didn't want to move. Every time I began to doze off, I would wake because of muscle spasms in different parts of my body.

Dieticians tried to coax me to eat 1,800 calories per day. A ridiculously large amount for a small almost immobile person. The advice usually went like this – You need to eat all of your food. 1,800 calories to help you get better and nourish your body...Blah, blah, blah. – The first few days' servings consisted of gelatin and broths. I really like gelatin, but even that I could not finish. Gradually, firmer foods such as fruits and fish were served. I never did finish everything.

On the sixth day, my temperature was decreasing but still high. I would sweat it out at night and when the nightshirt became uncomfortably wet, I rang for the nurses. Twice they helped to change my gown, as I could not manage that alone.

Each day, the nurses would take blood samples. By this time, my veins in the crook of my arm had collapsed. Further samples were taken from the top of my hand. My condition was improving slowly. I could now raise my left leg independently without help from my arms. Previous to this accident, I experienced light headaches only if something was wrong or if I was sick–which was a rare occasion. Throughout the hospital stay, I had constant headaches. I do not recall if they ever checked me for a concussion.

Although there was another patient in the two-bed room, we were in no condition to carry on a conversation, nor did I care to. My bed was by the window, but I never looked out. Television did not interest me. Between sleeping, and care giver visits, the days and nights were full. My psyche focused on getting better and after seven days of being in the hospital, I wanted out. I wanted to do things, see my friends and get back to normal. I could walk fairly well now and did not need bathing assistance. I could take care of myself at home. Nick had medic emergency training and I could rely on him if something went wrong.

Most of my friends worked but my good sailing buddy Mort Miles was retired. He lived on his 40-foot Choy Lee docked at the Alaskan Way public piers, and spent many days sailing. Hopefully he would be home. I called him and asked if he could pick me up. I did not want to take a cab and a bus ride would have been too rough and long.

On the eighth day, in the early morning, I discharged myself, against the advice of the nurses.

Mort, a good friend and a jolly fellow was just the right person to cheer me up. He thoughtfully brought a bouquet of yellow roses. The ride home was bumpy and although I still felt the jolts internally, I was so happy to be out of the hospital and talking with a close friend. I knew the early discharge was the right choice for me.

Prognosis

On follow-ups, the doctors told me that I would be fine. "You are healing well. Within the year, you will be back at playing baseball."

"I don't play baseball."

"Well, what do you play?"

"I sail, play tennis, roller skate, bicycle."

They assured me that I would be able to do all of that in no time.

Hmmm. Lies, speculation, and false hope.

Doctors try to be upbeat and encourage patients to get better but life is certainly not the way it was before. Trepidation overcame me when I tried physical movements as before. Can I jump as far? Row as hard without pain or injury? If not, then there is the extra time spent in healing and coming up to speed, if you can.

I certainly felt different in a couple of ways after the accident. The scar on my belly happened to be in line with pant zippers. I wore a bandage for at least six months to eliminate chafing.

The incision had cut muscles, and they had to heal before I could undulate the muscles in that area. The scarring forever restricted movements that previously I so easily performed in belly dancing.

The oddest sensation was that I was not myself. With three units of other people's blood flowing through my veins, I felt that an unfamiliar being was coursing through me. There were other people's hormones, DNA, and lifelines in my body. I wondered about the person or persons. What were they like? What were their personalities like? Would I take on some of their characteristics or inherit any disease or perhaps gain better immunity? What actually changes when someone else's lifeline is in you? I asked my roommates and other friends if I seemed the same. Was my personality the same, was I acting myself? Did I look different? No one suggested any differences, yet I detected some uneasiness in their responses. They said I looked and acted the same. Everyone seemed to want our interactions to be back to the way they were before my accident.

I was grateful that people donate blood. Without that generosity, I might not have lived. My dad gave blood every year, sometimes more often. When I lived in New York, I wanted to do that as well, but my weight did not meet the minimum requirement of 110 pounds to contribute. Finally, in my early 20s my weight was over by two pounds, just in time for a blood drive.

The doctors' reports stated, in their opinion, that I would be physically disabled for a three-month period and should not return to work within that time frame. However, I felt that I could sit at work, be productive and earn money rather than sit at home without a paycheck. Against the doctor's recommendation, I decided to return to work and found the workdays to be long and tiring. I worked in a city transportation department where most of the workers were on 24-hour call. There was a couch in the lady's room where I was able to rest and sleep during breaks and lunch. Those respites got me through the first few months after the hospital discharge.

The fact that I was not able to participate in some of my favorite activities, resulted in a slower and more cautious lifestyle. I also thought, why exercise? Why do anything when life can be over tomorrow? What is the use? Did I exercise all those months in order to survive a motorcycle accident? If I build myself up again will the benefit be in order to enable my body to survive another accident or illness? What would I do now?

These feelings took over a year to subside. Month after month, slowly, I believe that my own senses were regained. But not fully. What I was before the accident began to blur as I tried to reconcile my new physical and mental self with what I thought was another being in my body.

I adapted to participating in more passive sports, such as sailing, but I never did get back on my motorcycle again. I suppose that having been a trauma patient, I have PTSD. To this day, when I am a passenger in a car and there are motorcyclists near, I become a little tense and on alert for potential lane changes, potholes, and distance to the motorcycles. I always warn the driver, "Watch out, there is a motorcyclist in that lane."

5 *Dashed Ocean Dreams* *

Rolling Stones – "You Can't
Always Get What You Want"

Little did I realize that one of my favorite songs from 1969 would speak to me years later.

Big plans had been laid and I was but a small contributor. The 31st Bi-Annual Transpacific Yacht Race was to begin on July 3, 1981. This event was the 75th Diamond Jubilee of a popular sailing competition that began in 1906.[2] Seventy-five boats would sail from Los Angeles, California to Honolulu, Hawaii and culminate off the Diamond Head lighthouse. I was invited by an acquaintance to sail on one of the committee boats for this Transpac race, to help navigate, and stand watches. Our role was to have extra equipment for failures and monitor the boats in the race. Although I was fairly adept at navigation and handling most vessels from dinghies up to 110 foot tugboats (I had experience in sailing and racing in Puget Sound, Lake Washington, Lake Union, and passing through the Chittenden Locks), this was the first time I would sail a small 41 foot motorsailer on an open ocean. This voyage would be about 2,225 nautical miles for an estimated eight-day journey. For me, this was a once-in-a-lifetime event. Freedom on the open ocean. I had scheduled a two-week vacation and was totally energized looking forward to this adventure.

The flight from Seattle to Burbank, California took two hours without incident. My hosts, Jerry and Ed, met me at the airport and then gave me the Hollywood tour. From our car, we viewed the beautiful and expansive homes set into the hills in Hollywoodland. Ed pointed out houses in which movie stars lived.

After the tour, we began a land excursion to outfit the boat with supplies. Cartloads of food were brought on board to feed a crew of four.

An evening farewell party was held at Bobby McGee's, a popular disco in town. This was proven to me as bodies undulated on the dance floor, and laughter and movement filled the premises. During the party, Jerry, my acquaintance, became overly oppressive and possessive of me. Apparently, he was becoming fond of me and his intentions for my participation in this event were becoming more personal for him. His jealousy showed as he glowered at everyone in our party when I danced with others. Nothing was said, but his attitude made everyone in our party feel a bit uncomfortable.

We overnighted on the boat and the following day we continued to get the vessel into ship shape.

Ed, the captain and owner of the committee boat managed the pre-sail preparations. He had an agreeable personality and he and I worked well together. Jerry, however, must have had a full head of steam from the night before. His expectations were 180 degrees from mine. As his controlling temperament surfaced, he started treating me as a child. Jerry knew that I had more knowledge and boating experience than he did, yet he pushed more commands. He followed me around the ship monitoring my every move. Everything had to be done his way and I countered him on everything. Where the tools were to be stowed, and in what order, how the bed was to be made, on and on....

Although a man of few words and quiet, he became a talkative nagger. As this type of relationship was not on my agenda, tempers flared and I started to pack my gear. I did not want to be put into a situation where there would be many disagreements with Jerry on each move I made or didn't make. Jerry then appeared to be at odds with himself as he tried to back off on giving orders. He struggled on lessening his attempted control as he did not want to lose the battle on trying to control me nor did he want to tighten his control further and lose me and my crewing skills altogether.

I explained to Ed what was going on. "Look, Ed, I know how to organize supplies and tie lines. I don't want to be subjected to fighting with Jerry on each move I make or don't make."

"I understand. I felt the tension in the air between you and Jerry. Can you work out a compromise?" he asked.

Although Jerry was conflicted about whether I should leave, Ed was sorry to have me go. A capable crew of four was needed for the voyage. They would have to find another person that day. Even though I had more experience and sea time than Jerry had, Jerry and Ed were long-time good friends. There was no question that if someone was leaving it would be me. Also, there was no question that if I stayed, once we were out in the middle of the ocean with no escape, I felt that Jerry would become overbearing. That scenario made my decision. Jerry's mouth dropped open when I turned to leave and Ed turned to Jerry with his hands up and exacerbated, "We have to find another crew member today!"

I thought, 'Good riddance!'

I did not have a clue as to where I was going.

Leaving the dock, I did not turn around. I left the ship, surefooted and indignant. My solid plan to cross an ocean became an unfulfilled dream. Due to uncompromising personalities, here I was, alone. I felt stranded, in an unfamiliar town and not knowing anyone.

Well, I was not about to forfeit my first trip to California by giving up and immediately returning home. Although I walked away from a once-in-a-lifetime experience, I felt that being in sunny Newport Beach, one of California's most desirable cities should not be a short visit of three days with the last day holding a negative memory. I could have returned home to Washington, but what of my adventure? To drop my dream and plans like that? Absolutely not. A salvage mission was in order.

The Search Begins

While I contemplated some strategies, I enjoyed the beginning of a pleasant walk along the East Coast Highway overlooking the marinas. It was 105 degrees Fahrenheit. Luckily, the humidity was low, a dry heat, which felt like 80 degrees in Seattle. There was a gentle offshore breeze coming from the deserts on the east. Warm and dry as compared to the Seattle cold, moldy mists that I gladly left behind. The weather and views of hundreds of sailing vessels were inspirational enough to propel me forward intent on securing another crewing position.

After walking a few blocks, my boating shoes caused some blistering on my noncalloused heels. So I bought a pair of walking shoes and then proceeded to the docks to inquire at large sailing vessels if an extra hand was needed for the race or if they were hiring. The marinas were full of large sailing vessels. Many of them were being provisioned for the race. I walked many of the piers chatted with sailors while scrutinizing the vessels for size, apparent sea-worthiness, and the number of crew. While I knew nothing of the beach town, I knew boats and thought that I could have my pick of the best even though I had no money to contribute. I remained optimistic and longed to be part of a crew to participate in the Transpac.

Two well-known sailing ships, which I knew of from sailing in Seattle, Criterion and Spike Africa, were docked and provisioning for the Transpac race. What a stroke of luck if I could crew on one of them. Unfortunately, they did not need an extra hand as they had full crews. By one o'clock there was one possibility. A 30-foot Balboa, a single-masted cruiser, needed an extra hand for the race. Being disappointed about the size of the vessel-I hoped for something larger-I did not accept right away and continued my search as I felt more hopeful that there might be other possibilities.

After a while, in the late afternoon, I came across a 77-foot schooner. The skipper stated they needed someone for their charter business. Pay would be 300 dollars per month plus extra for chartering and I could live on board. Calculating out costs of rent and utilities, the net income was more than I was earning at my insurance desk job in Seattle. This sounded promising. He would confirm with the owner and get back to me on the next day. Great!

Decisions! Yah! I was elated to have a chance to fulfill my reason for coming to California in the first place. Here were the opportunities to take the sail of a lifetime to Hawaii and actually race in the Transpac or stay on in beautiful Newport Beach working and living on an old wooden schooner.

I hoped to find a larger boat than the Balboa in order to salvage and fulfill my ocean sailing dream, so I continued to inquire at other vessels, but no other positions were offered. After about eight hours of walking and making inquiries, my day was over and I had to find a motel.

Without much money and no credit card, I booked into a little no-tell motel a couple of blocks north on the highway. The room and furnishings were well worn yet smelled and looked clean. The door lock was a simple in the doorknob key lock. By myself without any real protection, I placed a heavy upholstered chair against the thin paneled exterior door, took out my folding knife and placed it under my pillow. If anyone got in, at least they would have a fight.

Around 1:00 a.m. I was awakened by the sound of the door knob jiggling and a thud as the door hit the chair. I heard male voices. Fully alert and aware that a break-in was in progress, I was immediately on my guard. I got up, knife in hand. The chair was heavy enough to prevent the door from easily being opened further. Did someone have keys to open the door? The door jiggling had stopped and I walked to the window to see two short, slightly built, men nonchalantly walking away. Taking their time like the act was business as usual. They continued past other rooms without trying the doors. Perhaps they worked at the motel and had seen me entering my room alone earlier that day. I will never know. At least I felt secure that the chair would hold any further attempts of intrusion.

The rest of the night was uneventful and due to exhaustion, sleep came quickly and was fairly restful.

The next day I returned to the schooner and found Skipper Bob at work cleaning the deck. The skipper seemed to have an affable personality and was not much older than me. He had conferred with the schooner's owner about my proposed employment. In addition to a monthly salary, there would be extra pay of 45 dollars for each charter plus tips.

A handshake and I was hired! I accepted. Great! Salvaged! Marine school had certainly prepared me for working on any vessel. How delightful it would be to sleep onboard each night, listening to the soft bell-like sounds of rigging tapping in the wind. This opening was unexpected and would not have happened had I not been determined and assertive. This was certainly a change in direction to a new alternative adventure. I had a new dream and sensed that this was going to be the most exciting summer job of my lifetime.

Crewing on Samarang

Samarang was built in 1932. A grand old wooden schooner owned by Ardeshir (Ardey) Bahar, a local architect. The layout was typical with the owner's cabin at the bow with a half bath, followed by a full galley. A bulkhead separated the galley from the settee which converted into a double berth. This open area also contained six bunks, and an enclosed three-quarter bath. A four-step wooden ladder led to the deck and cockpit.

Most of my days were filled with cleaning, vacuuming, shining chrome, washing the decks, sanding, and varnishing or painting. I became friendly with crews on other vessels in the marina and when extra help was needed, they hired me to prepare their boats for charter. On free days, my time was spent exploring areas such as Fashion Island, Balboa Island, Corona del Mar Beach, and Laguna Beach.

For the majority of the charters, we would sail roughly 26 miles into Avalon Inlet located on the southeastern shores of

Catalina Island. Depending upon the weather, wind speed and direction, passage took about three and a half to five hours. Compared to the motorized Catalina Flyer ferry which made the crossing in 90 minutes, this was a laid-back cruise. No rush, with time to throw a fishing line or lay back for a tan and view the seals sunning themselves on the buoys. Occasionally a whale's waterspout could be seen in the distance. We were never close enough to identify the species but suspect that they were Blue Whales. California's state marine mammal, the Gray Whale, migrates in the winter. Blue Whales migrate year round and are likely to be seen close to shore where we spotted them.

The crossing was most enjoyable with steady winds and the ship under full sail. However, there were times when the seas and winds were calm and the only way forward was by motoring. During those calm sea days, when halfway to the destination we would shut down the engine and drift. Those who were swimsuit ready would jump overboard for a no feet on the ground deep water swim. Captain Bob would throw out a line for safety and lower a ladder for swimmers to climb back on board. With no land and no other boaters in sight, this was the most private and largest pool to fool around in. Being in our own private universe was an awesome experience.

Samarang's draft required at least a ten-foot depth. The water was too shallow at the docks off Catalina Island. Therefore, we would anchor out in Avalon Harbor, lower the dinghy and transfer the guests onto a dock at the shore. The best part of anchoring out was the ability to dive overboard for a refreshing chilly swim. The water in Avalon was cooler than along the beaches of Newport and Balboa Island.

On July 10th, in preparation for an important charter, I repainted the interior of the dinghy. Not an artistic job, but at least the appearance was bright and clean.

The passengers, a film director and his wife arrived. Ardey might have had hopes of having his ship used in one of their films.

There were heavy seas that day. A rough ride caused the vessel to pitch and roll. Unfortunately, I had to go below into the galley and cook. I was hardly experienced in that capacity; after all, I was hired as a deckhand. Yet there I was at the ship's lowest point, three-quarters of the way forward, without a porthole to look out of. The galley area was tight and square allowing me to lean back against the counter while flipping burgers on the range in front of me. Yet the rolling and pounding wave action made it difficult to keep my balance. The heat from the stove did not help my queasy stomach. I struggled to breathe the moist stagnant air. Between serving courses, I kept running upside for air to reduce my nausea.

'B-r-e-a-t-h-e!'

I have never gotten seasick, even in rougher seas. This was my first ever sensation of extreme queasiness, but at least I did not vomit. I must have looked green as the captain and passengers were looking at me with anxiety and by 1400 hours they were beginning to starve.

Again, I thought, "Breathe. This cannot get worse. I cannot fail my probation time D-e-e-p breath." On each run to below and above.

Over an hour to make four simple meals of salad, hamburgers, and French beans. Perseverance paid off and the meals they consumed were satisfying.

By late evening, we finally arrived at Catalina Island and tied up to a buoy for a restful night on calm waters.

That evening, thankfully, Bob the Captain took the cooking chore over with barbeque on the beach. He cooked one-inch thick steaks perfectly charred lightly on the outside and slightly pink and tender on the inside. We concluded the evening by playing word games.

The next day we motored to the Isthmus at the western part of Catalina where many bison could be seen grazing on the hillside. Bison were brought to the island for a film shoot in the 1930s and then left behind. At one time Catalina was inhabited by 3,000 Tongva/Gabrieleno peoples. By the early 1800s, few natives remained as they became plagued by the measles and other diseases brought in by the Europeans. In the early 1900s, Catalina Island was owned exclusively by the Wrigley Company. The Wrigleys later granted about 88 percent of the land to be managed by the Catalina Island Conservancy. Today (2020), the island has about 4,000 inhabitants. A walk-on permit is still required to set foot on the island and the total number of vehicles restricted to about 1,000 for resident use only.

The sail back to Newport Beach was perfect. The waves kept pushing the stern over and Captain Bob found it taxing to keep the rudder over. With steady winds at about 20-25 knots, the crossing time was three and one-half hours. We made great time and enjoyed a fun sail.

The passengers must have enjoyed the voyage and weekend because they tipped me 50 dollars! I was surprised.

July 15th – It was nice to have the day off to explore more of Newport Beach. We were docked a mile and a half from the little Balboa Island Ferry that cost a mere 15 cents. After a brisk walk, I boarded the ferry for the five minute crossing to the landing on Balboa Peninsula. Balboa Boulevard, the main drag on the peninsula, was lined with souvenir, t-shirt, and sport rental equipment shops. Avoiding this very touristy area, I skipped on over to the oceanside for beach relaxation. Then a return trip on the ferry and a walk back to Samarang.

The crewing job worked out. A two-week probation period passed and so had my scheduled vacation time with Pemco Insurance. My decision was made. I could salvage my ocean dream. I flew back to Seattle to get my car, resigned from my job at Pemco Insurance Company, drove back down, and looked forward to a life at sea.

Life on board was very sociable. The majority of the sailors that I associated with were great fun, nice respectable fellows. Thinking back, I do not remember meeting any women workers. The women in California seemed to be interested mainly in the fashionable side of being onboard. Prancing or dancing on deck in the latest summer attire with a cocktail in hand. All of the lighter fun activities are understandable. But for me, being onboard ships is like floating on a cloud. Every bodily movement due to soft wave action is a slow motion dance in itself. Regardless of activity or weather conditions, every step is soft and cushioned on a wooden deck. The tinkling of the rigging sounds like chimes. Any disruption to the peacefulness is like a hammer to a metal gong.

One night I heard that hammer. A sharp clank on a winch. A dull stomp on deck. These were not typical nighttime sounds. Those uncharacteristic sounds woke me from a deep sleep. I froze in the bed, laying low under the solid side bunk rail. Maybe the intruder would not see me. Another couple of stomps and the cabin door opened. His outline was backlit and I let my guard down when I recognized him as a crew member from a ship two docks over. Daniel was an alright fellow, tall, slender, and not half-bad looking. He was about my age and we got along as friends and coworkers. When his captain needed an extra hand to prepare their vessel for charter, I worked with Daniel on the preparations. He entered the cabin and began to descend the ladder. What brought this entry on?

"What are you doing here? Is something wrong on your vessel?"

He mumbled something that nothing was wrong, but he wanted me. He started coming up the ladder to the top bunk that I slept in and he had amorous ideas. Oh, brother! Another relationship that I was not about to venture into.

"Get out of here!"

He continued to climb up and managed to get halfway into the bed. I gave him a good shove with arms and legs. It wasn't too difficult and I was able to force him out of my bed, as he was a bit stewed.

"Okay, okay! I'm leaving, but you are missing something."

Sure, I thought, yes, missing some good shut-eye.

The cabin never needed to be locked and I never did lock up. Strangers just never came onboard. I always felt safe here.

The next day, I told Bob about the incident. "Last night, as I was sleeping, Daniel tried to get into my bed. He was very drunk."

Bob was livid. It just so happened I saw Daniel walking down the pier to our ship. To avoid him, I went below to finish my breakfast. As he arrived, Bob jumped onto the dock and confronted Daniel before he could open his mouth. Bob told Daniel off right and left. "What were you thinking? If you ever try something like that again, you won't be working on any of the vessels in this marina!"

Hearing this, I came up the ladder to sneak a peek if a fight would ensue. Daniel put his hands and arms up in surrender and mumbled some apology. Needless to say, nothing was ever tried again.

The next day was spent preparing for an overnight charter for eight students celebrating a college graduation. This would be a beer keg party and the passengers would disembark on Catalina for dinner and check out any nightlife.

On the day of the charter, 12 party passengers showed up. The ship contained sleeping bunks for 10 people, still, Samarang could accommodate. A few young people, including our crew of three, were agreeable to sleeping up on deck. The sky was clear and sunny with soft breezes in the harbor. Sleeping on deck would be spectacular under the stars. A few graduates seemed more than thrilled, anticipating perhaps uninhibited romances.

We shoved off at 1330 hours. Winds were beginning to pick up so we reefed the main sail. By 1700 hours there were 40 mile per hour gale-force winds and seven-foot waves. Higher waves broke over the bow. Eight passengers were sick, three of them like dogs. I was not one of them. Not even a queasy stomach.

Captain Bob was at the wheel and I was working the sails. The ship was practically into the wind and we were not making much headway. In preparation for stronger winds, the main had been reefed. I was running forward getting ready to take the genoa down when a gust ripped the straining sail. I was able to take it down while Marcel, the other deckhand, took the foresail down. Together we took the main down as well. We motored slowly the rest of the way.

Distress call! We picked up a 40-foot sailboat that had lost its engine and had one sail remaining. We hooked up and towed them to Catalina. The sailboat named "My Delight" was then towed out by shore patrol to anchor out as the buoys and docks were full. Many boats were in distress and rather than return to the mainland and risk capsizing in the storm, boats anchored as close to the harbor as possible for protection from the blustery weather and seas. Some were too close. "My Delight" was probably renamed at some point to 'My Destruction' as they eventually lost their anchor, collided with other boats, and finally hit the rocks along the shore.

We chose an area with sufficient swing distance from other boats. Captain Bob lowered the bow anchor and the chain went off the windlass at the very end! Samarang had never been anchored at this deep of a depth before and the line had not been secured. Our bow anchor was lost. With only one anchor out, and seas still rough, we could not risk a collision with another vessel. Anticipating a probable situation where anchors would drag or the storm intensify, Bob, Marcel and I stood watch two hours each. Our anchor dragged a bit, nevertheless, it held. The storm eventually subsided.

I stood the 5 a.m. to 7 a.m. watch. The storm was over by that time. A relaxing uneventful quiet time at sea to watch a west coast sunrise, which I found to be not as nice as an east coast sunrise which rises above the Atlantic to greet the day shimmering reflective light over the ocean. I watched the sun as it rose over the western coastal towns. Sunlight trying without success to penetrate the haze of combined pollution and steamy evaporation from yesterday's rains.

Even though the seas were calmed, after experiencing yesterday's rough ride, four passengers went ashore to take the ferry back! They were done with sailing and did not want to gamble on the possibility of choppy waters on the sail back.

I believe that, the mere thought of swaying onboard on calm seas, would cause them to turn green.

As for Samarang, the storm's fury still had an effect. Upon weighing anchor, the anchor stuck on a 20-foot exposed telephone cable line. We cut our line and lost another anchor. We knew that Ardey would not be happy to learn that two anchors were lost.

Out of earshot of the guests, I joked, "Captain! We'll have two fashionable couples walk the gang-plank, for our bad luck." Captain Bob just rolled his eyes.

The return crossing to Newport Beach was smooth. There was a slight breeze and the sun was shining. Midway we cut the engines to take a dip in the warm ocean. The passengers were grateful for calm weather. Overall, they enjoyed the weekend party, experiencing both wild and stagnant seas. They were all excited about relaying stories of their weekend graduation party to friends. Back at the dock, they were even more elated and grateful to have sure footing on solid ground.

Upon learning that both anchors had been lost, Ardey turned red. "Before the next charter we are going out to find those anchors, or it's coming out of your salaries!"

There would be no overnight charter without an anchor.

Ardey wanted his anchors found. Later that week, we returned to the area with Ardey, Bob, and Marcel. All three went diving to search for the anchors. They found one anchor and also brought up some abalone and lobster. Bob prepared their catch in a frying pan with butter. They raved about the fresh taste of clean shell food, but I was apprehensive. This was my first taste of abalone and the taste was like lobster, except the texture was chewy like rubber. It was not worth a second bite.

My roommate telephoned me while I was in Los Angeles. "The owner has given us notice. They want to move back into the house. What shall I do with your furniture?"

I was so disappointed to hear that I would have to leave my floating home paradise on Lake Union. "Penny, please move my furniture, find an apartment for us and I will return soon."

Occasionally, Ardey would invite his friends and we would sail or motor at sea for a few hours or go to one of the many restaurants that had dockage. Most of these sailings were relaxed and free from tension. Certainly, the weather was always fine with sufficient breezes to usually put up the sails.

One afternoon we were motoring back to the home moorage. Captain Bob was at the helm and I was at the ready with a line to jump onto the dock to pull the stern in. Marcel was at the foredeck. An airstream began to move the stern away from the dock, which made me apprehensive with the distance I would have to jump to land on the dock. How far was that? Three feet?

"The dock is too far. I can't!" My heart rate increased. Would I land in the water between the hull and the dock? Now about four feet distance? As a kid, I beat others at the standing long jump, with no dire consequences if I failed. There was solid ground under my feet. This was an entirely different scenario. Visions of me underwater with the boat correcting itself and floating back to the dock over me entered my mind.

"Jump!" Captain Bob screamed, as he stood fast at the helm while the stern port side was swinging dangerously close to another docked vessel.

I did not want to be the one responsible for a collision. This was no time to linger as the distance continued to increase.

Heart pumping heat into my face, I set my mind to complete my task at hand, beginning with a long leap. A deep breath. I do not know how it happened, but suddenly my knees bent. And with an adrenaline inspired jump I was in the air as the stern continued to move away from the dock. With short legs and a longer torso, how far can an untrained five foot two inch person jump from a standing position?

Every day I learned a little something more in order to live and love my new experiences. Success! Both feet landed, heels on the edge of the dock with a solid sure-footed thud. Releasing my breath, I could breathe again.

With line in hand and my mindset calmed and focused on accustomed tasks, I moved rapidly to pull the stern in close to the dock in time to prevent a collision.

I met many wonderful people working the charters. The crewing was not all hard work. There were a lot of fun times, a chili tasting contest on Catalina, lots of swimming and best of all...

The Ancient Mariners Race[3] *August 2nd, 1981*

Another weather perfect day, on August 1st, 1981 we sailed off from Newport Beach at 1500 hours to participate in the Ancient Mariners Race. The race is named not for old worn-out sailors, nor for the undead spirits of the 'Long-lost Evil Race', but for classic old wooden schooners.

We arrived in Long Beach at 2100 hours and buoyed in the harbor overnight. Although it was a bit late, we made time to visit the RMS Queen Mary, a historic ocean liner built in the 1930s which was conveniently docked within a few minutes of our buoy. Skipper Bob lowered the dinghy to ferry ourselves over. We toured the ship and had a light dinner in one of the many restaurants onboard. By midnight, five of us psyched-up sailors, were back onboard Samarang.

In the morning, we were thoroughly rested and prepared for the competition. I was confident in the ship and our abilities to work as a team to be winners.

The race began at 1332 hours. Winds were light and consistent at about 15 to 20 knots, pushing us smoothly through the waters. The course was within the harbor and buoys marked turning points. We were making great time holding second or third place, with sails close-hauled and the toerails skimming the water's surface. I was holding my own on a winch with occasional help from a tailer. Captain Ardey was at the helm all through the challenging three-hour race.

The harbor seemed to be at capacity as there were many close maneuvers. Schooner Medley was rammed by a larger vessel. The resulting hull damage caused them to drop out. Captain Ardey showed his skills during one close call when the same large ship that rammed Medley maneuvered to thwart our course causing a slight reduction in our speed. We theorized that we would have placed second had this not happened. While listening to the race results, we discussed filing a protest against the offending boat and possible penalties for the captain who manipulated so aggressively to stay on his course. We mused that a good flogging and being forced to walk the plank was decidedly a more appropriate punishment; however, the ideas were left to the air currents as all of us were running on euphoric adrenaline.

Dancing on deck ensued. We were so excited and about to jump out of our skins. To cool off, four of our crew members crammed themselves into the tiny bath and showered in cold water. Other celebratory actions included toasts with a bottle of champagne. At the end of the day, we were still pleased that we placed 5th.

The Ancient Mariner's Race was the culmination of my summer activities in California. Other sailing races in fiberglass boats do not compare. To be part of a small crew competing against other historic wooden schooners was a living history experience. Having crewed in the Ancient Mariner's Race and on Samarang more than made up for not participating in the Transpac open ocean crossing.

By the end of September, Ardey was reducing the charter business to schedule more sailing time for his personal use. He informed me that I would have to make other arrangements for board and full-time employment.

The friends I made in Newport Beach wanted me to leave Seattle and make Newport Beach my permanent home. Bob's girlfriend, Maureen, worked at a local newspaper company and stated there were job openings. Another of my dreams could be fulfilled by working as an assistant editor for a periodical. Housing was solved also as her roommate recently moved out and the share in her apartment was available. The offerings were so tempting and the timing so right.

In three months, I had crewed on 30 charters; met and made more fun and generous friends, than I had in iceberg Seattle over a two-year period. How could I leave my new friends and my new Italian boyfriend? He was divine. With a Cary Grant persona he had beautiful, dark brown hair, light brown deep eyes, and standing about five foot nine inches he was not too tall for me. He treated me as his queen. I had a future here. Living in a sailor's paradise could be extended indefinitely. My future in Seattle was not set. An open road was before me. It was difficult to choose between reapplying to my dead-end, yet secure, insurance job in cloudy Seattle or embarking on a new adventure working for a newspaper company. The thought of totally giving up my comfortable living arrangement in Seattle didn't appeal to me at that point in my life. Nor could I support two separate apartments.

In the past, I had never regretted leaving any of my abodes. I always looked forward to the future, change and better times. And this was a better time. Would I regret abandoning a sun filled life by returning to Seattle?

My southern friends continued to entice me to stay by taking me out to lunch and other great offers. "I'll set up an interview for you at the newspaper."

"You can stay on-board Samarang until my roommate moves out next week."

After considering my options, I took the easy choice. My sense of responsibility won out. The economics of keeping a shared apartment in Seattle while working in Newport Beach was too wasteful according to my philosophy on life and thriftiness and too extravagant for my marine-oriented lifestyle. The dream of a 'jet-set' lifestyle would have to wait.

In two days, I would return to Seattle.

With free time to enjoy the area, I drove to Laguna Beach to check out the Sawdust Art and Craft Festival–a fair of local artists and musicians. And one final visit to relax on a wonderful California beach and enjoy warm waters and sand.

The drive back on I-5 was uneventful yet interesting to me, a city gal who had never seen the horizon on land. My eyes scanned an expanse of acres of golden pastureland in California. Then an unappetizing view of a dairy farm appeared. One hears of crowded conditions, but this was startling seeing thousands of black cows trapped behind barbed wire fencing and crowded into delineated farms, standing in black mud and sludge, shoulder-to-shoulder and rump-to-rump. I wondered if cows feel as trapped and confused as they look. They do not have much of a choice.

Humans have choices. Reviewing my summer, I was pleased with my decision to leave the committee boat. I would have been trapped on a 41-foot vessel for over a week, on an open ocean with an overbearing crewmate. Now I was beginning to feel confident about my choice to return to Seattle. Back to familiar friends and territory. New adventures could be made in any town.

Update

Upon returning to the land and a new living arrangement, I drove to my new address. Penny did secure a lovely large apartment located in Ballard above a newspaper print shop. We were on the second floor with access to a deck on the roof above. It was quiet and private not having neighbors next door. The print shop started early in the morning. The low-level noise wasn't bothersome as we were both early risers.

That arrangement ended, when her boyfriend moved in. They eventually married and I moved out. The same friends, whom I lived with when I first arrived in Seattle, let me stay in their spare bedroom in Ballard. The house was a 1920s framed home with a working washer and dryer of the same vintage. The dryer had a hand roller wringer. The machines were simple and worked well. A half hour of washing and my exercise routine was complete. It brought back memories of my great-grandmother using a wash tub and board. She was fit and healthy without wasting time on aerobicizing.

Through no interference of mine my roommates, Diane and Nick, began having marriage difficulties and separated. Diane and I moved out and then shared a two-bedroom 1970s apartment located also in Ballard.

In 1982, the population of Seattle was under 500,000. It was not unusual to see some of the same faces on the bus or walking the streets every day. About once a week, I would walk along Alaskan Way on a raised sidewalk which parallels Puget Sound and visit friends who moored their boats at the public pier. Wooden piers jutted out into the sound supporting shopping malls that catered to tourists and locals alike. My friend Mort docked his 40-foot Cheoy Lee sailboat at the public moorage near the Pier 52 ferry terminal. If he wasn't there, I would lunch at Ivar's Fish Bar on Pier 54 while watching the seagulls beg for a French fry or two.

It was just one of those days the following summer after my crewing summer in Newport Beach that I ran into the fellow who had invited me to crew on one of the committee boats for the Transpac race. Jerry was walking towards me along Alaskan Way by the Ye Olde Curiosity Shop. I hadn't thought about him and neither of us had made any attempt to call. This chance crossing presented an opportunity to hear about the voyage and whether or not another person had replaced me. I was anxious to know.

Jerry appeared genuinely pleased to see me and we made plans to have lunch together the following week.

During lunch, the conversation immediately turned to the previous summer. "Did you ever find someone to crew?"

"Yes, someone walking the piers came onboard. She wanted to get to Hawaii. She didn't have any navigational skills and basically was learning throughout the crossing."

"Well, did she get seasick?"

"Oh wow, did she turn green. A lot," Jerry laughed.

He showed pictures of the arrival in Hawaii and other party events. He was soft spoken and here, showed no signs of authority. As Jerry relayed minimal information about the order onboard, he didn't seem to have been pleased with her seamanship skills.

I supposed that Jerry was in his element giving orders and that she did as she was told, assuming she understood any maritime terms.

The 1981 Transpac race turned out to be the greatest in Transpac history. Even though steady winds throughout the race did not exceed 35 knots, there were many exciting moments. Some of the highlights included: one demasting due to a collision on the way to the start line; a few vessels had equipment failure during the race and had to drop out; two men went overboard and were rescued during one of many rain squalls; and to top it off–a new Transpac record daily run of 304 miles. It was a race that was talked about for some time.

6 *Adventures in Travel*

Prior to 9/11, travel was fun. There was a thrill in being transported thousands of feet above the earth. Passengers were polite and neatly dressed. Airfare was expensive compared to today's prices. If the flight was turbulent, passengers applauded and cheered after landing safely.

The destination is the reward and usually the best part of travel.

Hurricane Iniki

"Through meteorology, we know essentially how hurricanes form, even though we can't say where the next storm will arise." – Eric Maskin

One of the tropical islands we enjoyed exploring for its diverse temperate climate was Hawaii's island of Kauai. The northern portion of the island is cooler and wetter than the southern dry and hot Poipu Beach. We were vacationing mid-island by the eastern shores of Wailua Bay at the Hilton Garden Hotel. For three lovely sunny days, we snorkeled and walked miles on the beaches.

A distant storm was taking form on September 5, 1992. On Wednesday, September 9, we snorkeled most of the day and I had to beef up my snorkeling skills as the wave action was stronger and the ocean waters had become turbid and unduly churned up. There was a chill in the air and the skies had an eerie light grey tone. A much different atmosphere than what we typically experienced in Kauai and what we had enjoyed the few days prior.

That evening Joseph expressed that he had an uneasy feeling and wanted to cut our vacation short, as he felt an ominous dread for the upcoming days. "I really want to go home. I have a sense of foreboding. I can't put my finger on it, but I am very uneasy."

"But Joseph, we have paid for our stay. There is no refund." I did not want to go home.

It may have been uncomfortable for him but frugality won over.

The next day, the Thursday evening news stated that a tropical storm would be headed easterly towards Kauai. Meteorologists predicted that the storm would pass north of the island, which alleviated any concerns that vacation plans should be altered.

Our room was dark on Friday morning. With no light streaming in through the curtains, we overslept until nine-thirty in the morning. At that time, the maids were knocking on doors asking guests to bring in lanai tables and chairs, and to close the curtains. We did so, then dressed and went downstairs for coffee.

Palm trees were bending in the breeze. Joseph noted, "Winds are picking up. The waters will be too rough for snorkeling today. I guess we will stay by the pool." We agreed to have a low-key day.

Guests and staff in the lobby all seemed to be in a hushed mood. After breakfast, a voice over the intercom system solemnly stated, "Attention Guests. The hotel will be evacuated. A bus, parked at the entry will be available to take you to a shelter away from the estimated trajectory of the storm. There will be two trips. One at ten thirty and one at eleven fifteen. Please do not take anything with you as there isn't space for luggage on the bus."

Kauai Community College, located eight miles southwest of our beach hotel, was situated at a higher elevation of about 360 feet. Huge tidal waves were expected so local weather watchers and hotel staff assumed the higher elevation and inland location would be a safer area than near the beach. We were uncertain about taking the bus and decided to drive our rental car for more independence in returning to our hotel.

Some of the evacuees had radios and Hilton employees kept us informed. The news reports recommended that stores close by 11 a.m. and that everyone plan to stay off of the streets. Winds were at that time 35 miles per hour with gusts to 60. By 1:00 p.m. gusts had escalated to 85 miles per hour. Winds were blowing horizontally, all afternoon. Metal flashing and light poles were flying about. About 20 people were courageous and stood outside under an entry overhang and watched the storm.

Several small separate buildings made up the college campus. We were all in the Nursing building. Soon the roof developed leaks and then the windows blew out. The cold and slightly damp floors were now wet from rain dripping through the ceiling. We were lucky to have a generator powering lighting for hallways but not for bathrooms. There was no running water for the toilets. Hilton security relocated us to a gymnasium type building that was still in one piece.

By early evening, we were so grateful that Hilton provided dinner. Staff set up a buffet-style dinner with sandwiches, meats, fruits, and vegetables. Some people were real pigs, hoarding food as if it were their last meal. We waited our turn in line and took only what we could eat for dinner.

The National Weather forecast was off the air, having lost connectivity around 1:00 a.m. We found it difficult to sleep all night long. Others spent time talking, singing, and joking. There were no pillows nor blankets. Only hard plastic school chairs to rest on. A few evacuees had the foresight to bring some bedding. Joseph and I remained quiet and to ourselves curled up on the cold tile floors trying to catch a snooze. Unable to do so, we went into the empty Science Lab building. Joseph laid down on the tables and I wandered looking at telescopes, Petri dishes, and periodic tables that hung on the walls. Even with the warmth of the air, surfaces were cold and damp from humidity. On the positive side though, not to hear constant jabbering was quite a relief, as we were the only occupants in the building.

Sounding restless, Joseph said, "I can't rest," as he slowly turned and slid off the table.

"Why not?"

The detailed scientist in him explained, "I am concerned that there may be chemical residue from science experiments still remaining on the surface."

Due to that worry, we returned to the gymnasium. Small groups huddled against the walls. A few played card games to pass the time.

I have always hit the bed running, then collapsing into a heavy slumber anywhere. Nights are usually restful; but not tonight. The floors are cold and the shifting winds keep us awake amid the echoed chattering laughter. Spending a night in a community college hallway was not the vacation we had planned for.

We sat on the bare tile floor in a hallway that had double doors at each end. At one end of the hall the double doors, although closed and locked, were pounding as if a monster were trying to break the doors down. Then suddenly everything went dead quiet for a few minutes. Not a sound. Everyone inside stopped talking. We wondered perhaps if the storm had ended. We went outside for a brief look. Above, the sky was clear and dark. Surrounding us was a light cloud. We realized the stillness was not the end of the storm but we were looking at and were in the eye of the storm. I was spooked with shivers and we quickly returned to the hallway and then heard a quiet whistle of a breeze that quickly escalated in volume. Then just as suddenly the doors at the other end of the hall started to shake and pound. This slamming continued throughout the night.

Torrential rains came again. At three in the morning I ventured a walk outside staying within four feet of the relative safety of the building. In the silhouette of the night, we could see that most trees and large shrubs were denuded. Minimal leafing remained on the branches. Light poles down, roofs blown off, metal scraps everywhere. It was a shocking sight.

By early morning, the hurricane had passed and we left the shelter via our rental car. Most cars in the lot were damaged. Busted out windshields and back windows. Some convertible tops were blown off. We lucked out with our rental car having sustained minimal damage to the right front fender, antennae broken, left rear view mirror was gone, and a few minor scratches.

On the drive back to the hotel, the scenery was like an unfinished jigsaw puzzle. We weaved around debris and lost landmarks. Some street signs, structures and homes were completely gone. A sugar cane field flattened; hillsides denuded; evergreen trees, if standing, lost most branches and needles.

We tried to make sense of the surroundings. "Wasn't there a house there before? What street are we on? Watch out for the downed electrical line!"

All power poles and lines were down. Some of the poles, and trees that had been blown across the road had already been sawed into smaller pieces and set over off the roadway.

Compared to the many devastated structures, our hotel had little damage. Many windows were broken, and the three swimming pools were filled with debris from trees and awnings. Cars left in the parking lot were safe and most without damage! The hurricane had changed its course, skirted the hotel and blew directly over the school. Who could have foretold that it would have been better to stay at the hotel?

The once expansive white sand beach was now washed away. Rough waves hit the bulkhead, bringing broken branches and other debris to decompose on the darkened brown shore.

As electricity was needed to pump water, the restroom facilities did not flush. Our hotel room was located on the third floor of the hotel. We hadn't filled the tub with water before leaving and now we used the wastebasket to get water from the debris-filled swimming pools to flush the toilet.

Breakfast was provided by Hilton. Since there were no generators to keep refrigerators working, waiters brought out anything perishable to be consumed first. We had our fill of bacon and other meats for two days. Even though no one knew how long we would be stranded we did not worry about a food supply.

In the southern area of Kauai, some of the hotels in Poipu were uninhabitable due to severe damage. *Jurassic Park*, the movie, was being filmed here at the time. Several of the actors and film crew were booked into hotels on the southern part of the island and they were able to fly out first, some by private jet. Another group from our hotel also volunteered to fly out by helicopter. As Hilton was the most habitable structure on the island, the evacuation plan relocated Hilton guests out first allowing military and news media personnel to move in and occupy empty rooms while others slept in the lobby.

While other hotels abandoned their guests and lost their staff to worries of their families and to make immediate emergency repairs of their damaged homes, Hilton staff continued to work at the hotel. Even the bar was open. They did their best to make guests comfortable. The evening bartender smiled and was cordial as he made our drinks. We were concerned for him. "How is your home and your family?"

"My home is gone." Without missing a beat, he smiled and continued to work the bar. "I can stay here at the hotel and have a roof over my head."

And such was the situation of many of the staff. They were fortunate that they could work and sleep at the hotel if they needed to. They all remained professional and helpful to guests, considering their plight.

On Saturday evening, 100 people from our Hilton Hotel were signed up to be airlifted out by the military so that emergency personnel, reporters from the media, and military could occupy their rooms. The helicopter landed behind the hotel. We didn't take the airlift due to uncertain timetables in connecting with commercial aircraft and there would be no reception to meet us in Honolulu. Reports stated that a light storm was rolling in and we did not want to fly in heavy rains and strong winds. We were told that the earliest estimated time that we could then leave might be two days later in the afternoon.

On Monday morning, we decided to sign up for the second flight of 100 Hilton evacuees to be flown out. The first 100 left the hotel the day before at 9 a.m. to be flown out by a commercial jet. We thanked our lucky stars that we signed up for the second flight because the first group was supposed to have flown out on Sunday at five in the afternoon but instead had to stay the night at the small airport. Electricity was still out and with no running water, they relived the night spent at the community college, sleeping on plastic chairs or the tile floor.

The following day eighty-six of us boarded two buses and arrived at Lihue Airport at 11 a.m. We stood in a long wait line outside and slowly moved forward with our luggage. Luckily the weather cooperated with a bright, clear sun and a slight breeze. All airlines cooperated by sending any available planes. TV reporters at the Hilton and airport took pictures to document their reports. We were finally seated on an airplane and the Aloha flight took off at 3 p.m. to Honolulu. There we would transfer to another plane to Los Angeles.

Hurricane Iniki had dissipated halfway between Hawaii and Alaska so the flight home progressed without issue. We arrived safely at the Los Angeles airport. The Red Cross was there to provide relief in the form of food and a coupon to take a shower in a Minute Suite in the terminal.

After the long wait to board the first plane off of Kauai and then the transfer to another plane in Hilo, we were in a trance like state still trying to reconcile the images of the past few days and the luxuries before us. We could finally relax as we stepped into the shower. The small cubicle was immaculate and contained a small cot, shower, sink, and toilet with flowing water. It was a transition back to civilization. The little bologna and cheese sandwiches on white bread filled our stomachs. We were grateful that an organization like the Red Cross was there to help us.

We later learned that over 14,000 homes were damaged and about a quarter of the population-about 12,000 people-lived in public shelters after the storm. The eye of the storm traveled for 40 minutes over the island of Kauai with gusts in some areas over 200 miles per hour and sustained winds at 150 miles per hour, it was classified as a Category 4 storm and one of the most damaging storms to hit Hawaii.

The following year, in 1993, the movie *Jurassic Park* was released and included some of the footage from the storm. I wonder how different the movie might have been if the hurricane hadn't shortened the film production on the island. Today, tour companies will guide visitors to five locations, on Kauai, that were in Jurassic movies.

Tourism, businesses, and residents did not recover for several years. We returned five years later in 1997. While many facilities were renovated and reopened, many hotels were left abandoned.

To this day, I carry a flashlight in my purse and pillows in my car. There have been two occasions to use the flashlight and both occurred while I was in a windowless public restroom.

7 *The Working Life Reinvented* *

You Bought What?! *

Overtime, physically, I healed fairly well after the motorcycle accident and I continued to work in a transportation field office as a dispatcher. The work also involved timekeeping, filing, walk-in counter assistance, and acting mother/sister to approximately 30 male workers.

Mentally, I still desired a more diversified job. To accomplish that goal, I took real estate classes in the evening. I planned to transition into sales and was becoming familiar with forms and the general real estate market.

Tom worked in the same building as an electrician in the electrical shop. He was a handy do-it-yourself home project type of fellow, yet never in a rush to do the work. He would often tell me of his home projects. "The paint is peeling on the south side of our house. I'll paint that side this summer. Next year, I will remove the moss on the north side and paint the first-floor level." Everything was done in stages, much to the disquietude of his wife. They lived in an older area of Seattle in the same house for decades. They were planning their retirement life which would be a year off from 1984. Both wanted a change of scenery; to see a forest rather than an asphalt street, to relax, and for Tom not to work on every broken-down appliance or piece of hardware in the house. Having a new home by the ocean would satisfy their idea of retirement life and they scoured elevated ocean-view lots near the Ocean Shores area of Washington.

One day he sauntered into my area in his laid-back casual way, "Say, Heather, would you take a look at this real estate purchase and sale agreement?"

"Well, I am not an expert. You may want to have an attorney review the document, but I would be happy to preview it for you."

He handed me one piece of paper. An official real estate land purchase and sale form. Contracts were short and sweet in those days, but this was really short. I began to read each word carefully and chuckled after the first paragraph. Proceeding through to the end, it took just a few minutes.

"So, what are you buying?"

"It's a nice standard sized lot, about 12,000 square feet, one block from the ocean at about a 140-foot elevation."

"Oh, that is great! By the time you move in and become settled, in a few years you may own waterfront property as the glaciers slowly melt and the water rises," I chided. "It will be a good investment." I became serious again. "Well. All the blanks are filled in, but nowhere does it read that you are buying a vacant lot. You could be buying the Brooklyn Bridge for all I can tell. Those 15,000 dollars would be a great deal for a bridge, but maintenance would be exorbitant. How would you afford it? Not to mention the flying time to the east coast."

Tom stared at me blankly, waiting for an explanation.

"I understand that this is a rural area, but contracts should include a description of what you are buying. As there is no street address for your vacant lot, a legal description is needed. Other than that, the document looks good to me."

"Thanks! Good point. I'll get back to the sales agent and have her insert a description."

Contracts have evolved and have become lengthy and much more complicated since that time.

Tom bought that lot, and a small self-sufficient camper to sleep in overnight.

* * *

During the 1980s, the yuppy decade was a time of reinventing myself physically and mentally for stability. As I grew into my late thirties, I began to seriously reflect upon childhood dreams. What did I really want to be and do for the rest of my life? And where did I want to live?

I was growing up, becoming a more mature adult and had a nice paying-nine dollar and fifty cents per hour-entry-level job. Becoming tired of moving I wanted my own place and bought a 1950s daylight basement rambler home in North Seattle. Satin finish revealed the beautiful warm colors of solid oak floors and wooden mahogany cabinets. Tongue and groove soffits in the eaves were also unpainted oak. Two bedrooms, a full bath on the first floor, and in the full basement a bedroom, three-quarter tile bath, recreational room plus a bonus room, and another room off of the utility which I turned into an efficiency kitchen.

The most beautiful and healthy Pacific madrone tree was outside the back corner of the house. The adjoining neighbor did not like the 30-foot-tall tree and wanted it pruned. He also argued for a complete removal, complaining of bark and leaf debris. I would not allow any pruning. Why damage a perfectly healthy tree? The tree and all limbs remained for the duration of my ownership.

A couple of years later the real main man came into my life. He did not want to live in Seattle and I sold my wonderful house. I am sorry I sold that home as a lot of sweat went into that property without reaping the equity.

I moved into his 900-square-foot two-bedroom 1979 condominium in the Overlake neighborhood of Bellevue. He wanted more room and even though I liked the cozy size, we bought a three-bedroom new home in the area. The house had a wonderful unique layout. A soaring angled entry with corner windows and three skylights that all brought in lots of light.

Living in a new home brought ideas of improving my employment situation to a more professional vocation.

My husband would say, "You are such a grasshopper. I am an ant. Slow and steady."

Actually, I was more like a squirrel and would hide my treasures to save for a rainy day. I thought and traveled more like a butterfly-chaotic, no straight path, yet my journeys always led to the end goal, and sometimes to the dining table. When we first met, I was about 29 years of age and had already worked eight different jobs. None held more than three years and at the time, after five years, I was not happy in the dispatch position. My supervisor relied on my work. When hearing that I had intentions of finding employment elsewhere, he provoked, "Ha. You are not going anywhere."

I was not to be resigned with resentment. After that statement a restless flurry of resumes were sent out to other divisions handled by the same personnel department. All applications were rejected except for one which was far below my pay scale, to which I rejected the invitation for an interview.

It was time to change course and analyze what professional vocation would bring satisfaction. The old rhyme 'Tinker, Tailor, Soldier, Sailor ...' came to mind, but none of those classifications fit me. The field of real estate had always been of interest, yet I had never pursued it. Probably due to the misdirection of my youth as my father discouraged that vocation. As 'maturity' was setting in, I continued taking real estate courses. One topic was of particular interest-appraising. In my early youth, I had considered myself to be nonjudgmental, unbiased, and extremely objective with the ability to see both sides of an argument and then come to an equitable solution. These were some of the traits needed in an appraising profession. There were several specialty areas of interest, but the question was-which specialty would be most lucrative. Jewelry? I adored jewelry and wore a lot of white metals and stones. Two good friends were jewelers and one was a diamond cutter. They taught me the basic knowledge of certain characteristics to look for in quality stones.

Estate appraising? That would combine my loves of both personal property and real property. However, with personal articles owners would certainly attach too much sentimental value to inherited items. Values change with fluid lifestyles. This area of appraising seemed too volatile.

Real estate was grounded. In my thirties, my determination and stamina were the forces needed to break into a field that men typically pursued. Women were considered to be too emotional and biased. I was neither. The vocation was probably in my genes. My father was a real estate broker, as were his father and grandfather. I believe that I had the genetic makeup for it.

To begin this career, one would apprentice under an MAI (Member Appraisal Institute). After completion of a few pertinent courses and many hours of field appraisals working under a certified appraiser, the apprentice would be eligible to take a state examination and if passed, a license is issued, and then one is qualified to sign their own appraisals.

Several local appraisal companies were listed in the phone book and I contacted most of them. My solicitations and requests for information or an interview were rejected, often with a tone of scoffing dismissals. These offices were apparently closed to female applicants. This was during an escalating real estate market with generous refinance and mortgage rates. Banks and independent appraisal companies were busy and actively hiring. After several rejections to apprentice under an MAI, a co-worker of my husband recommended a small company in Burien. The owner was beginning a class for potential apprentices under his tutelage.

I called the owner, Mr. Peone. He said yes, he would be glad to include me in his training class. This was my break.

He operated out of his home with his office in the basement. When I arrived at the address he had described over the telephone, I was not sure that I had the correct location. In place of a business placard on the door, a sign with an arrow pointed to the side yard. The yard was overgrown and the house in disrepair. As I walked down the sloped side yard, I was quite apprehensive about the quality and reputation of this business. But after so many rejections, I was desperate to get into this field and out of an office dispatching job.

Mr. Peone was a big towering man, possibly 300 pounds or more and one of the nicest men I have ever met. I did quite well in his course. He hired me and he favored my work, much to the consternation and jealousy of the three male employees.

He had high standards. Investors and banks appreciated our detail and honesty. We never lacked for assignments. I worked for Mr. Peone for a couple of years as a real estate appraiser and continued to expand my knowledge in the real estate field by taking classes in construction and law. Soon I was working and studying six days per week. Joseph was not keen on my long absences and irregular hours. We both wanted more vacation time and I wanted a job with a steady pension. The search was on for that easy government job my dad always advised on.

The Spy Who Wasn't *

All peoples have their own unique way of living in their home castles. Safe within and behind their walls, the residents feel secure that no one is aware nor the wiser for seeing their idiosyncrasies and eccentricities. Passersby and friends may never be invited in.

But there is a stranger who is uninvited and sometimes unwelcome. One who does legally enter many homes.

Like an actor who learns his lines and character development, I practiced a dialogue, got into neighborhoods and learned its people, their habits, and desires. The job was to gain access into homes quickly and elicit information as rapidly and efficiently as possible. And I excelled at speed and acquiring information.

Suspicious residents thinking that I might be casing the neighborhood would stop me and ask who I was and what I was doing. Others called the police and on more than one occasion, I was stopped and informed by the police, "We have a report that you have been seen looking into windows."

The residents called me 'trespasser', 'spy', 'tax collector', and 'voyeur'. Indeed, I was none of those. To refute each description, I will explain.

Trespasser? No. According to the laws of the land, I had enforceable rights to inspect property.[3] If the owner continued to deny access, then the Department of Revenue might get involved to assist.[4] A court-ordered inspection might be required if a property owner continued to refuse entry-but in my tenure and memory of historical events, that process had never been considered necessary. There were other nefarious ways to obtain information.

Spy? Well, perhaps just nosey on my part. I obtained information by looking into windows. Sometimes occupants pretended to not be at home even though they were clearly visible from the outside.

On one such occasion, after knocking and ringing the doorbell, no one answered. Maybe someone might be in the backyard. I walked to the back yard. Clearly visible through an uncurtained window were a young couple engaged in conversation. They paid no attention to my knock on the window. The person washing dishes did not acknowledge me nor pause their conversation.

Voyeur? No. Just doing my job. Like a speed-reader, I captured a picture of the scene and remembered it for all time.

Tax collector? No. No money exchanged hands. The payments come in the form of high tax bills when in truth, the democratically controlled tax system, pushed a simple majority to raise taxes. In many counties, the highest percentage of property taxes paid was to public school systems. As an

---

[3] RCW 84.40.025
[4] RCW 84.08

example, in 2018, 56 percent of the total tax bill in some taxing jurisdictions was allocated to public schools. In 2022, the percentage may have been as high as 62, even though the schools were basically closed for two years during a coronavirus health crisis.

Part of my job was to measure new construction and homes that were being remodeled with new additions. I made a contest out of a day's work. If a co-worker was with me, we raced to measure, collect data, outline, and enter specs into the computer system. We didn't run for a prize, we simply laughed and enjoyed our day. (Yes, I took after my dad. My work was my play.) In a typical cookie-cutter residential plat, the maximum number I could measure was eight. For custom homes with angles, turrets or half stories, the time frame could be up to one hour to measure and draw one home. For the most difficult designs where a home might be built into the hillside or perhaps was not accessible, there were building plans that could be used, however, field checks and verifications were required.

Lots of equipment had to be carried. Aside from the 'uniform' of hat, sunglasses, boots, and gloves, I carried a Polaroid camera and extra film (pre-electronics era), clipboard, flashlight, 100-foot reel measuring tape, mag light, binoculars, rags, identification tag, hand towels, face mask, paper map book (GPS was not a standard issue), all the accoutrements for lunch and snacks, and dog bones to detract an aggressive animal. Pepper spray was not authorized although it was needed and carried by some. Management, by office judgment, determined that dog bones would suffice for all aggressive confrontations. For other emergencies, in the city we relied on Good Samaritan neighbors. In the country, we were out of luck without a cell phone. When electronics came into play a laser measuring device was used to measure interior rooms.

For eighty percent of the four-day work week, my older car served as my office. The air-conditioner was pathetic and could not cool the vehicle when temperatures were over 90 degrees. Blue ice packs kept my arms or legs from burning up.

We proceeded with caution into every neighborhood and property. An identification placard was placed on top of the car's dash in the event I was illegally parked or blocking another vehicle. If the neighbors assumed that a prowler might be in the neighborhood, the placard would indicate that the 'prowling' was legitimate.

We never knew who the owners or renters were in the homes. Our office gave notice to the local police departments when we were out inspecting each and every unit in older neighborhoods. On one typical afternoon, my task was to look at every single property in a residential area. One street will never be gone from my memory. I drove down a semi-improved cul-de-sac without sidewalks and street lighting. Tall fir trees bordered the roadway and driveways on the individual lots. The 1970 era houses were set back from the street and built on larger lots each about a third of an acre. This was a typical middle-class street. My paperwork highlighted a couple of houses that needed to be inspected for remodeling status or condition changes. One property was flagged as requiring a condition check for possible remodeling in progress. I was still in my car as I peered down a long tree-lined driveway to the subject building that was visibly in need of a little TLC. However, there was something else that I noted. Something was not right. An eerie atmosphere emanated from this home and property. It was an unclean sensation. A feeling so uncomfortable came over me overpowering my confidence and responsibility to inspect the property. Contradicting my usual assertiveness, I did not drive down that driveway; I didn't even attempt to turn the steering wheel, anticipating that I might have to drive away quickly.

At this time in my career, I had inspected over 5,000 properties. This turns out to be about 1,200 per year. I had come to experience that all properties, even vacant lands have an atmosphere. Or one could say homes, houses and land can give off an aura, they have souls. The offing may be one of well-being or of consternation. New construction is an exception as a clean slate, a new home is empty and typically void of these characteristics.

Whether or not a house is occupied, vacant, a drug house, or transitional, an older property will project an impression. Lives are lived; memories are made. A house becomes us. Not only are our styles and personalities reflected by the home, but also our essence.

There is a reason why we hear of houses that are occupied by ghosts. Over time, residents become attached to their homes and do not want to leave them. They become part of the home. I am not sure how personalities emanate from houses; I simply know that I can feel they are part of the home.

I was unnerved by the mysterious atmosphere that emanated from the suburban home that I did not inspect and whenever I thought about that scene, that feeling of uneasiness returned. It was not for a year or two after I avoided inspecting that property that a news story identified a long searched-for serial killer. Since I had worked extensively in the town, I was curious if the killer's house was one that I had been to. A shiver ran through my body as the suspect's name showed as the owner of the property where I had made the decision to keep driving. Had the owner been home, one can just imagine what might have happened had I entered.

This was the dream job I had hoped for? The building we worked out of was considered to be unsafe for its past use as a school. The electrical panel was underpowered and couldn't carry one fan to circulate the hot stifling air in the summer. The roof leaked in several areas through asbestos insulated ceilings. So, yes, I relished working outdoors, unconfined to four walls. Working (playing) outdoors was the type of atmosphere I longed for all my life. And finally, arriving at midlife, I was able to achieve that.

Working outdoors and in unfamiliar neighborhoods can be risky. Each day brought a new challenge or escapade. Although I was exposed to toxic chemicals, calmed angry property owners, watched from a second story window as a driver drove into my parked car and took off, chased by dogs in the city and by horses in the country, and viewed goats stomping the hood of a car; each interaction was dealt with by having a logical open mind and the encounters prepared me for the next unscripted act. I learned new things every day, lived through the day and loved the excitement.

Sometime thereafter, I applied for an upgrade. The position required more office time on computers analyzing sales, and reviewing staff work. As providence would determine destiny, my interview occurred on the same day as the Twin Towers attack.

With the Twin Tower crash and my dear friend, Nick who worked there, in mind, I knew I answered questions correctly but with less enthusiasm than would have normally been displayed. The head of the department was encouraging, but the lead supervisor actually fell asleep! I should have not wasted my time. The opening did not fall to me, but to an inexperienced co-worker. Seniority certainly did not work in that interview. Naturally, I was upset that the promotion was not offered to me.

The by-pass turned out to be fortuitous, as the upgrade required being in an office 80 percent of the work week. Time spent typing into a computer, working on charts and calculations. Tasks that I was good at, but did not bring the stimulation and adventure that I craved. Only being in new situations, meeting new people, and being out of doors would bring satisfaction. Although I didn't realize it at the time, it was to my advantage that the promotion was awarded to another co-worker. The way the interview was handled and the resulting rejection provided an incentive to seek advancement elsewhere.

Real Estate Services Come Together *

Everything one has done, leads you to today.

My goal was to stay in the real estate profession, yet I liked to think outside of that box and for creativity the children's rhyme-Rich man, Poor man, Beggar man, Thief, Doctor, Lawyer, Indian Chief-kept resurfacing in my thoughts. I also reviewed my past positions. I was all over the place in real life. Cashier, tele-marketer, coat/hat checker, clothing sales, personnel, employee benefits, inventory, accounting, sailing crew deck hand, insurance agent, dispatcher, Master Gardener and tour guide, real estate agent, appraiser.

I evaluated what I enjoyed most and the one characteristic that was necessary for me was freedom of movement. The conclusion I came to was that all of my skills could come together in managing real estate. After a few interviews with various government and private agencies, I was hired to maintain an inventory listing of thousands of government-owned lands. Vacant lands would be actively managed. My background as an appraiser and real estate sales agent worked to manage and sell these lands via auction or direct negotiation. A background as a Master Gardener and classes in Forest Stewardship came in handy while I inspected for tree health, water issues, and grounds maintenance. A background in insurance worked in investigating claims of damage from water seepage, drainage issues, and trees falling on cars.

During one big storm, a young fellow called to report that a street tree had fallen on his vehicle "Is this claims servicing? My car was parked on the street and the wind blew a tree across the hood of my car, damaging the windshield. What do I need to do?"

"You should contact your insurance company. Such damages are typically covered under comprehensive."

He sounded disgruntled, "I don't have any insurance. Who is going to pay for this?"

"If you have not purchased insurance coverage through a company, then you are insuring yourself. You are responsible for paying to repair any damages."

Past experience as a tele-marketer prepared me for rejection. Learned skills in persistence and doggedness paid off. Due to my experience in appraising, sales, and skill in assertiveness, I was promoted to Right-of-Way Agent. Here I would value lands and present offers to purchase private land for public use, such as for easements, roads, drainage ditches, and replacement of bridges.

The job was awesome. Right on the cutting edge of what would be happening out in the transportation world before the general public would realize what was happening. All requests for new roads, major repairs, and full property management of thousands of government real estate holdings came through this office. We were in the know, delving deep into hidden sub surfaces, secrets of property owners, and always researching and unearthing what lay beneath the surface-not only in real estate ownership, but also in people's faces. Knowing the desires that lay behind their masked façade was an advantage to direct solutions to make the project tick and be successful.

My perspective as a real estate agent was different from the engineers who designed the infrastructure. The engineers were focused on one goal-getting a certain number of pedestrians and vehicular weight across roads, or designing a fish culvert to handle the flow of water to enhance fish migration. I had to see the whole picture-from within the box to outside-how the project might affect future owners, their neighbors, and the public.

On one such transaction, after several attempts to negotiate with an estate representative, the owners hired a land use real estate attorney to represent their interests. The attorney was a tough one with a record of winning many court cases. After I exchanged several telephone calls and letters over a few weeks with this attorney my supervisor, Harry M., called me into his office. Harry M. a seasoned banker and manager could work the system if needed. He was also the fastest two finger typist in existence. There were no secretaries in the office. We all handled our own correspondence, phone calls, and schedules. For him to sound so serious caused concern. I thought, "What did I do now? Had I screwed up?" He had a Machiavellian smirk on his face.

"Heather, what did you do to Bob J? What did you say to his client? Bob J telephoned and told me, 'Take your real estate pit dog off of my client!'"

What? Quiet, push-over, level-headed, and timid, ME? I was level-headed, diplomatic in reactions and statements. Certainly, Bob J had dealt with tough, nasty negotiators. I was a walk in the park compared to others. Much later, I realized that Bob J had most likely bluffed, trying to intimidate me. It was all part of the negotiations.

The co-worker, who had trained me, was a seasoned real estate salesperson. Dotty was always successful in her negotiations. I wanted to emulate her technique, but I never was able to do that. Dotty was short, at about five foot-one. With hair shaved close to her scalp, her big beautiful white-toothed smile stood out in contrast from her smooth ebony skin. I watched intently as she negotiated. She was calm, yet forceful. She was ready with a quick big smile when her offers were accepted. If the owners showed any reluctance, she would open her eyes a little wider while still talking slowly and give what can just be described as a hypnotizing devilish stare. Ultimately, the owner would agree and sign the required papers.

Real Estate is an amazing structure—water, trees, buildings, and people help this all come together.

8 *Housing Searches* *

Walks Around the Block *

When shopping for a home and neighborhood one usually reflects upon the homey childhood memories of safe and enjoyable neighborhoods in which one grew up. For me, it was Rego Park. Rego Park was built on swamp land.

In the mid-1950s, my grandmother Claire would take me to Forest Park on Woodhaven Boulevard and in a sinister soft voice tell me not to venture into a low-lying grasslands area that was surrounded by trees because the ground was a swamp and I would be sucked down and not be able to walk out. Luckily, I felt safe with her and under protection from any evils that might await in the forest or emerge from under the muddy water.

In those days, the 'swamp' was named Hempstead Swamp and had many cattail type grassy plants. It has since been renamed Strack Pond. According to a view of aerial maps on the internet, the area appears to have water deep enough to be an actual pond.

Rego Park lies at the approximate center of the borough of Queens, New York. I grew up in a safe residential neighborhood known as The Crescents and lived there from the time I was five until I was 15. The homes were built in the 1920s, consisting mostly of sturdy two-and-one-half-story brick Tudors.

The Crescents was named such because the small neighborhood streets were laid out in a fanned crescent shape and were named alphabetically. The shortest street Asquith Crescent is followed by Boelsen Crescent, then Cromwell Crescent, Dieterle Crescent, and finally Ellwell Crescent. The sixth is not a curved full crescent as the two ends of the fan curve straight outwards and therefore named Fitchett Street. Every day I would walk these sidewalks lined with old oak trees and spend a good half hour getting from Point A (home) to Point B being the main commercial streets four blocks away.

My grandmother told me a little secret. She said that if I avoided stepping on cracks in the sidewalk, I would find money. This kept me entertained on my walks and occasionally there was money to be found. Typically coins or a dollar bill. One time my walk was more profitable than usual and I found a five-dollar bill. All of my financial finds I placed in my glass piggy bank or a small working toy cash register.

In front of each home stood one old oak tree in a narrow planting strip at the street side between the sidewalk and the curb. In the autumn, residents would rake the fallen oak leaves into two-foot-high mounds leaving them on the lawns. The mounds would later either be burned or put into garbage bags for the weekly garbage pickup day. So many mounds of leaves waiting to be kicked high into the air, back into the lawn and out onto the curb and sidewalks. What a delight it was to see the leaves fall again!

Yes, I was the culprit. The crisp autumn air tingled my face. My feet kicked the leaves high, and the breezes swirled them back down, brushed my face and left a dusty odor. Who could resist?

On warm dry days during the spring and summer, inevitably there would be an elderly or disabled neighbor sitting in a chair or in a wheelchair in the middle of their driveway. Some were reading, or dozing, or perhaps simply meditating. Even though they lived with their children and grandchildren they still appeared so lonely, hoping and anticipating that someone would stop and chat.

The neighbors knew most everyone within about a three-block radius. When people were out, there was always a quick greeting or short chat. One of the neighbors, a middle-aged man in a wheelchair, would be in the driveway and was always reading. He had multiple sclerosis. At first, I had difficulty in understanding him as his speech was affected by the disease. As time went on and I learned his language, it became easier to understand him and we talked about the books he read. He so longed to have conversation, but I always had somewhere to be and I found it difficult to end the interesting discussions, not only for myself but for him as well.

I often have dreams about the walks around the block. There must be something important and meaningful to me about those times. Now when I search for a place to be, I am always drawn to neighborhoods with large trees and older Tudor-styled homes.

As I contemplate this, the realization sets in that I am still going around the block and still searching.

Even when there is no plan to neither move nor remodel my search continues as I love looking at houses, especially underground or non-square homes. The design aspects are intriguing. I have designed a couple of homes to my specifications and enjoy decorating interior and exterior spaces. Entering a home, I understand the lifestyle of the owner and toss it aside. I visualize a room as vacant with monochrome-colored walls, and then my imagination goes on full blast with my colorful decorating schemes.

Unique Housing Searches *

Starting from scratch here is what one might need to know to site a house:

Not all properties are connected to a public water system. In that case, a private well needs to be dug. Therefore, it is important to know how to Dowse.

Dowsing technique: Use a V-shaped freshly cut flexible branch with all small twigs removed. Willow and maple are pliable and soft. The rod should be the diameter of a pencil and about 18 inches long. Hold each end at waist level with palms up and the wide V end three inches above your waist. Walk with even deliberate steps, do not shuffle, and do not raise your feet high. The branch will move vertically at a water supply.

Mark time by lifting your foot five or four inches off the ground. When the twig is vertical, that is the number of feet down to drill.

Strength of pull determines the flow. Just count.

In the early 1980s many vacant lands for sale needed to have a well dug, so I was prepared with that knowledge. Now I invite you to have a view of some of the more unique or eccentric homes, and stranger-than-you-can-know home decorating schemes.

Hoarders With Treasures

I was single and looking for acreage in the mountains, hoping to find a clean and remote site with a small cabin. The advertisement sounded promising. Five acres with a two-bedroom cabin accessed via a private dirt road. The asking price was too good to be true and below my budget. The bells should have gone off, but I was hungry for a home surrounded by forests. I took time off work to make the appointment, denying the possibility that a low price was the first indicator that the property was not what I hoped for.

I drove twenty minutes to the Issaquah-Hobart area and exited off Highway 18. The property was a few blocks away and easily accessed from the arterial. The long-curved dirt drive was carved out between tall evergreens and was shared by two property owners. This was the private setting that I wanted. The first home off the lane was a nicely maintained lodge-type styled house built around the mid-1970s. At the top of the hill, the topography leveled to an open clearing surrounded by a forest. I spotted a small owner-built wooden cabin. The owners were waiting for me. They looked like hippies from the 60s. "Come on in! Please take your time and look around."

The cabin fit my style with a low six-foot-high ceiling. The kitchen was in the center of the living room and although small it was well organized and equipped. A potbelly wood stove for cooking and heat stood close to the sink. Pots hung from hooks and space saving shelving served as a pantry. Quilt like soft curtains hung from slim rods over the windows and also separated one of the bedrooms from the living area. This home would be easy to care for and I could picture myself living here.

The owner then invited me outside to tour the grounds. The sign that I had previously ignored became quite visible. What came into view was a dump site. The owners hoarded street signs, barbecues, lawn mowers, vehicles, various deteriorated building supplies, piles of tools, two portable swimming pools, and treasures. All treasures. "Items can be sold. They are valuable," said the owner. "I can sell and get rid of the cars and most of the equipment and building supplies before closing."

Yeah, right, I thought. Clearing and cleaning up would cost as much as what they were asking. There is nothing like seeing other folk's hoarded piles to motivate the viewer to go home and immediately reorganize and eliminate a few household items.

At the end of the tour, on three legal-sized pages, I listed about 130 different items that had to be removed. Who can use six motorized lawn mowers or two riding mowers? Two Kenworth trucks, over 50 tires, 23 cars, five campers, a school bus, and 22 trucks, all in various non-working condition. The family was not that big. Their two-bedroom cabin was small, hobbit sized. Yet they lived large on acreage surrounded by forest and their useful treasures.

The Medieval

Some individuals live in another era. A large Tudor-styled castle, sited at the waterfront, was being remodeled by the owner. He was a middle-aged, single man with shoulder-length wavy hair that was uncombed. He wore worn jeans and an open plaid brushed cotton shirt over a white t-shirt. He seemed a little reluctant to let me in, but he submitted and led me to the garage first.

I was there to check on remodeling changes that were being made. The large garage was at a 90-degree angle from the house. Once used as an airplane hangar, the well-lit garage was now an art gallery protecting paintings. Thus far not so unusual. Many residents extend their living area into an attached or detached garage.

The arched front door entrance was overgrown with vines and ivy. The interior had large spacious rooms in a 5,000 square foot home. I entered into an open room living concept with dining, living and kitchen. There was minimal furniture in the living room, perhaps a small couch and chair. In contrast to the heavy timbered ceiling, a few inexpensive veneered kitchen cabinets hung on an interior wall. Counter space set off the small kitchen, which seemed to be an afterthought along a wall in a corner. The dark wood-beamed two-story ceiling would have been the envy of anyone if the great room was not so stark. Actually, the whole property could be someone's wet dream. Stepping out of the living room to the back patio revealed a long infinity swimming pool that appeared to flow into the bay.

Utilitarian iron hardware adorned heavy wooden doors and the straight iron balusters had a simple design with small round balls on every other picket. There was a mystery room he would not let me into. My imagination went wild. I wondered if behind the door was a sadomasochist dungeon with all the accoutrements of leather whips, chains, and collars. Recurring events tend to manifest as characteristics in a home's bones and furnishings. The emptiness seemed to echo sighs. This home exuded an atmosphere of an orgy delight.

Green With Envy?

Everyday can be a St. Patty's Day. Right? In 1993, my husband and I looked at a large 5,000 plus square foot home on Vashon Island which was still under construction. The home included seismic sensors, so sensitive that footsteps could be detected. Perhaps the sensors were part of the security system. Emerald green kitchen cabinets? Not for everyone's taste. Except on only one holiday per year, that green color is for salads and green beans.

Unfortunately we had not toured the home prior to the installation of the cabinets and primary colored mosaic tiles. The cost to redesign a brand-new kitchen was out of the realm for my frugality.

Even so, my frugality has its limits. For our lifestyle, owning a home on waterfront property could be a dream come true. With that vision in mind, we began our hunt for a home with an unlimited view. For some owners, though, that amenity can be an occasional nightmare.

Risk Takers

Some people like to live on the edge–continually. Excitement is never far from their door. Edgecliff Drive is appropriately named. Small backyards face the water to the west atop a 170-foot cliff. Beach access would be had if you could descend and climb like a mountain goat. Some of the owners did build trails and steps to the beach.

After six months of searching for a uniquely designed home near or on a waterfront, I was on the verge of despair. We decided to look at a design that I am not excited about, but it was on high-bank waterfront. The home we toured had a 1970s Northwest style with an A-framed living room. It was pretty typical except that it was built on steel girders. The apex projected two feet past the cliff's edge. The owner asked if we would like to walk the trail to the beach. We might have been looking at a quite steep 60 degree angle and we declined. He then told this story: He had been working on improving trail access to the beach when the hillside gave way. He went down with the slide and was buried up to his neck in the sand. The tide was out.

Rarely do people walk along this beach at low tide. During high tide, the water covers the sandy beach to the base of the cliff. I do not know how long he was buried, but he was being looked after. A lone couple happened to be walking on the beach! They were able to contact the fire department and he was rescued before the tide came back in.

His story cinched or decision. Should more of the land side, the tipping scale would be too much of a risk for us.

Finishing Touches *

*Every personal material object
holds the essence of our soul.*

In 1986, Joseph and I answered a For Sale by Owner advertisement. The owners were anxious to sell as they had accepted a job offer and were moving back to the East Coast. The price and description matched our criteria so we quickly made an appointment to tour the property before dinner that evening.

On the way to our destination, we drove through a six-year-old development in the north-end of the Bridle Trails area of Kirkland. Many evergreen trees, possibly planted 30 or more years ago, still stood, tall and healthy, which made the neighborhood feel established and elegant. The 1980s-era homes were well-kept with manicured landscapes. The street we were looking for backed up to a neighborhood arterial with small convenience stores across the street. A perfect distance for my morning walks to a coffee shop to read the morning newspaper.

We turned into a cul-de-sac and counted the numbered addresses. Further ahead one house clearly stood out. The house was trimmed with toilet paper strewn from the roof to the ground. Unfortunately, that was the property we were to tour. Joseph, who did not like resales with other people's problems to begin with said, "I'm not going in there. The interior must be a mess."

I tried, unsuccessfully, to stifle a few chuckles. "That is probably the result of a Halloween prank by one of the neighborhood teenagers. Other than the toilet paper, it looks like any other home on the street. Look, we made an appointment, we are here, and the price is good. Let's go in."

"Alright, but if this is a disaster, you owe me big time. Why I let you talk me into this, I will never know."

A straight concrete path led us to the front door where the owners greeted us and we entered into an open foyer facing a wooden staircase without railings. Only the metal footings remained.

"I love metal railings! Do you have the baluster?" I asked the missus.

"Yes. It is in storage. The iron balusters are an ornamental Italian style. We removed the railings, as we do not use such things."

My eyes scanned to the sunken living room on the right and bulged wide-open seeing white linens draping the walls in a circular fashion from the 12-foot-high ceiling to the floor. Large white panels leaned against some of the walls.

The owner explained, "I am an artist. This is *my* bed and the panels are my construction. They can easily be removed without damage to the walls."

Her queen-sized bed was at the far mid-wall. *Gee,* I thought, *I wonder where her husband sleeps.* At the center was a low coffee table draped with white linen. On top, set a large bowl filled with plastic bits similar to pieces from a Lego set.

With all the white linens on the floor, we could not step down into the sunken living room. *Hmmm.* I pondered, *Lovemaking in a cloud-like atmosphere?* The room looked like a set for a theater production without visible cameras.

Off to the left of the staircase was the half bath, adjoining the utility room, which also served as a craft room. The missus stated that one of her art projects was painting figurines. Multi-colored paints splattered the fiberglass sink and laminated counters. *Messy,* I allowed, *but not so unusual. A good-sized utility room is quite useful for various hobbies, such as sewing and painting.*

The missus led us through the short hallway to the breakfast nook and kitchen. I tried to keep my jaw from dropping and to keep from laughing. I dared not look directly at Joseph, for he is someone who has a hard time concealing his feelings. His reaction might have brought what I knew he was feeling out in me. I saw out of the corner of my eye that he was surprisingly straight-faced. His stoical expression prevented an outburst of laughter from me. How could anyone eat here? Paperwork in disarray covered the dinette table. Small boxes of toys and games were stacked on every chair. The counters were cluttered with ceramic plates, pizza boxes, stacks of paper plates, and coffee mugs. Dirty plates and utensils filled the sink. I considered whether they ate standing up or in the formal dining room.

The first floor was laid out in a circular fashion with a separate formal dining room adjoining the kitchen.

There was an entire server in the dimly lit dining room. Not a side boy nor server as in buffet, but a whole computer system. A VAX-11/780, which my husband was familiar with when working at Boeing in the late 1970s and early 80s. The size of it took up the entire room. Two other cabinets held the reel-to-reel magnetic tape drive. Joseph now showed interest and had a serious conversation with the owner about the setup. The mister was a computer geek and the dining room served as his office. I wondered if he slept here as well. Thick cables ran through a four-inch diameter hole in the floor to the crawl space. Ooo kaaaay.

That concluded the tour of the first floor. The owners stayed indoors while we went out the back to see an unkempt yard with more toilet paper along the deck rails and many empty plastic plant containers under the deck. Interestingly, there were few planted shrubs or perennials growing in the ground to show for the number of vacated pots.

Frowning with a clenched jaw, Joseph was agitated and wanted to leave. "Let's get out of here; I don't want to waste any more time. In this condition, no real estate agent would waste their time on this place. No wonder it is a For Sale by Owner!"

Nevertheless, I was intrigued. I had to see the rest of the house. "That would be rude. It won't take much longer to see a few more rooms."

We quickly returned inside and the missus led us upstairs to the second floor.

The master bath was filled with freestanding plastic shelving holding thousands of knickknacks and small toy figurines. Furniture boxes blocked full access so we could barely peer into the bathroom. The sink and tub were full of unpainted figurines. The owners bragged that the master bath was like new because it had never been used. The owner was not fooling me, even unused appliances and plumbing fixtures wear out. After years of non-use, gaskets dry up and would have to be replaced.

Of course we had viewed the bath by first walking through the master bedroom, which could not be visualized as a sleeping area. Being used as a storage area, the plain room was unimpressive. I wondered if any lights from the shopping center and parking lot might shine through the window but I was unable to walk to the window to check out a view to the garden and beyond. Boxes filled the room and another five-tiered white plastic shelving unit was filled with unpainted plastic figurines.

One bedroom was for the birds. Literally. The owners would not open the door because the macaws were not to be disturbed while sleeping.

Another bedroom housed cats. Joseph is highly allergic and I expected an unpleasant cat odor so we did not look into that room. Surprisingly though, with so many unwashed dishes, animals, and clutter in the house, we did not detect any bad odors. The house was not dirty nor was there an accumulation of dust.

There was one standard bedroom that was used by their son. He was sitting on his bed and reading. With his head still lowered, he looked up at us. He seemed embarrassed. Whether it was due to strangers peering into his space or due to his parent's decorating style, we could not tell. Decorated with posters of his sports heroes, it showed as a typical teenage boy's room.

We were not shown the second bath, nor did we ask.

I wish I had pictures.

At this point, we had seen enough of the partially viewable house and did not ask to see the garage. We thanked the owners for the tour and tried not to run too fast to our car. Needless to say, we did not make an offer on the home. We surmised that no realtor would list the house in that state. However, had the house not backed to a noisy neighborhood arterial, I might have made allowances for repairs and seriously pursued negotiations.

I respect individualism. Everyone makes their own style. For me, non-cookie-cutter homes attract me. The more oblique and curved the windows or rooms are, the more interesting. Picture a Hobbit house. That would be my little bit of paradise. However, when it comes around to selling, the majority of buyers like the mundane-square or rectangular rooms. A blank neutral canvas to visualize themselves in. I can look past unique decorating styles and see the bones of the building.

For Joseph, who does not like to house hunt, this menagerie of other people's decorating styles and living habits was all too much. It took the cake, the last straw, the coup de grace. During our three-month search, we had looked at two resales. Only two, yet he had reached his limit.

"I told you this would be a disaster. Why didn't we leave earlier? This was a total waste of time."

Backing out of the driveway and away from their view, I could not hold it any longer and totally cracked up laughing hysterically. "Oh, come on now. It was an experience! You will never see anything like that again. What do you suppose they do with all those unpainted figurines? What kind of episodes do you suppose they have in the white draped living room?"

"Grrrr. I would rather not know. Total waste of time. You are right; I will never see anything like that again. We are not going to buy that house."

"We could probably buy it at a discount." I teased. "A good value with built-in equity."

"No."

This was the last resale we looked at. From then on out we would tour only new construction.

The Exotic

Why are some strange habits in others sensed as normal in my life? On a garden tour, I happened to use a bathroom facility that was overflowing with plants. Plants in the bathtub, plants on the window sill, plants on the floor, plants hanging from hooks that were screwed into the ceiling and into the walls, plants on shelves, plants hanging from the shower rod, plants on the sink surround, plants on the toilet tank... need I go on? Did I miss a space? Oh yes, there were plants on a small table and hanging from hooks on the door. And these were not just tiny two to four-inch pots, some pots were a foot across with four-foot-tall plants, and all housed in a bathroom sized about eight feet by seven feet. Let's be kind and say that the air was clean and fresh.

Okay. Please be not be so surprised and aghast. Two years later, I am in a similar predicament. One hundred plants line our window sills. When my husband complained of the amount of time spent in caring for the plants and the amount of space they took up, I had to count them to believe him. Yes, I am addicted, and falling in love again with Old Man of the Andes-a fuzzy cactus, *Oreocereus trollii*. Who knows how long the attraction will last.

9 City Girl Moves to The Desert *

First Let's Glamp *

In our younger years, almost everyone had the opportunity to enjoy a hike or camping trip in the deep forests or at the very least at an organized campground. Amenities were primitive. Fire pits were used to cook meals, rivers or lakes provided water, and cesspools were utilized for basic needs. You learned the skills needed to survive in the wild should you become separated from your buddies or encounter aggressive wildlife.

It has been over 20 years since I have had the pleasure of sleeping out of doors. I admit that the contours of my body no longer cushion my joints and bones. These days I require excessive comfort and automatic remote devices to assist in mobility and dexterity. For me, tent camping is a bygone activity.

Living in a city, I missed the soft rushing sounds of rivers. It had been way too long since we experienced breathing unpolluted clean air and being in emerald green forests which refreshed our souls. Joseph and I ruminated over how we could recreate some of those past glorious camping trips without the high probability of bodily injury while setting up camp. Could we build a campfire without falling into the flames?

And, what about rising from a sleeping bag after a sleepless night feeling like rocks had been implanted into our backs? Mornings are my favorite time of the day. Would it take most of the morning hours to realign our joints in order to rise up out of a sleeping bag?

Our friends advised us not to Camp, but to Glamp. "Aaoh!" I thought, "Glamping, the answer to save our aching aging bodies." Glamping is the new adventure in senior outdoor recreation.

"Modern camping rigs have all the facilities available in a house. You can enjoy all of the outdoor activities without the hassle and work of pitching a tent," our friends told us. "All of your basic home comforts are at hand." A cozy adventure concept sounded appealing and advanced our plan to recreate past camping adventures.

With visions of reconstructing earlier camping trips but with the benefit of modern amenities, we were convinced that glamping would provide the serenity and scenery of the great outdoors while we relaxed in a luxurious all-weather recreational vehicle (RV). We would have our 'home', wherever we were. We set off to the nearest 'Living the Dream' RV dealership.

Our new hardcover 'tent' would be outfitted with air-conditioning. No more suffering from heat stroke. A small refrigerator to keep our food safe from bears and other wildlife and a freezer for ice cold drinks or ice cream. A propane cooking top to prepare gourmet meals. No more fire nor smoke hazards. The conveniences of indoor plumbing. No more worries about snakes or other wildlife encounters at midnight while walking to the loo. And to top it off, with a mere touch of a button, the cushy sofa converts into a four-inch-thick mattress laid on a raised flat even surface. Ahhh! No more rocks embedded in our backs. We would have wonderful restful nights.

In the winter, late-night huddling around a smoky campfire would be passé. We would have a safe portable smokeless propane fire pit, and in the RV a built-in heater. Dimmable mood lighting at floor level and above the overhead cabinets. With extra battery power and solar panels, we could boon-dock in the wild if we chose not to book a site in a commercial RV park. There were so many options and benefits.

We were in our 60s and due for a true change of life-style in our retirement years. A time for dreaming, reimagining, and moving forward to implement our dreams. A hard paneled 'tent' seemed the ticket. We signed on the bottom line, geared up and we were off planning our first glamping trip.

The first time we tried to reserve a spot on the Washington State camping website, we were overcome with choices and menu options. After a half hour, we found a site that fit our time frame. Finally at the checkout page. Failure. Another visitor had just taken our selection. After a few other failed attempts, we gave up and phoned the reservation line and waited on hold for an additional 20 minutes. Impatient! I want to get out on the road! I hung up the phone and we got on the road without reservations.

By 3 p.m., we arrived at a Washington State Park and snagged the last space available in the campground. The days of uncrowded parks are gone. Nowadays one needs an advance reservation to ensure a good site. Our first urban, faux camping experience was an eye-opener. Smoke from wood burning fire pits, barbecues, a distant forest fire, and cigarettes, chocked us and was overwhelming. Kids on big wheels were constantly screaming, dogs barked at every passing person, dog, or low-flying bird that ventured near their campsite. Massive 40-foot motor homes and off-road vehicles spewed diesel or gas fumes. Over-revved engines roared, as drivers attempted an incline pulling oversized trailers. There were more tents with power, than tents with bare necessities. Thus, 'campers' had their computers, radios, and porch lights turned on. Some motor homes sport outdoor television screens. Rather than waking to the sounds of birds in the early morning, we were awakened by a park's maintenance crew mowing the acres of lawn and a waste management truck emptying garbage containers. *Ahhh. Is This the Life?!*

"Oh, you have got to be kidding. Have we been transported back to the city? Joseph, this is not the experience we expected."

No natural wildlife, bears, coyotes nor deer were to be seen. Not even a rabbit. Campers brought the wildlife with them—dogs, cats, ferrets, or birds. On the *AHH* relief side, our joints and muscles suffered no harm nor stress as it is fairly simple to set up a recreational vehicle. Simply hook up a hose for city water and plug in an electric cord for power. However, my heart cannot take the new technological 'camping' lifestyle.

After a one night's stay, we were happy to return home. Yet a week later, the wanderlust began to surface.

Joseph was searching the internet and looking at maps as he planned our next outing. "We have technology! Thanks to the solar batteries, we are going to boon dock by a river."

Change your scenery and you can change your life. With two other motorhomes in sight, we spent two enjoyable quiet days by the Columbia River fishing, listening to the birds and watching windsurfers.

Our motorhome became our ship on wheels. Our favorite places to camp were by bodies of water. We made an unplanned overnighter, at an RV park in Crescent City, California. Our site was steps from the beach. Joseph asked, "Do you hear the foghorn? It will keep you awake at night."

"Are you kidding? This is my paradise!"

I slept like a log. The sounds of the seagulls and the foghorn were background music filling me with memories of floating at sea.

"Now, this is the way to *live our dream!*"

A Calculated Risk *

"Come to Arizona! Come to Arizona!" Our friends beckoned. From 2010 to 2018 many of our friends either wintered in or permanently relocated to towns such as Yucca, Sun City West, Surprise, Chandler, John, Phoenix, Tucson, and Fountain Hills.

Joseph and I were enticed and flirted with the idea of buying a second home in Maricopa County, near the Gold Canyon area. We thought of the convenience of having a small one-bedroom home with a large garage to park our camper. However, this type of dwelling was not available. The closest development with our required amenities was in Mohave, five hours away. We did not want to be that far away from our friends. Prices were reasonable in 2015, yet after much debate and consideration in maintaining a second property, we decided against it and considered our camper to be our 'second home'.

Fast forward to 2020-when the news stories were all about relocation and lifestyle changes. Perspectives changed due to the Covid 19 pandemic and self-imposed isolation. Many people relocated and two years later were still moving to the southern states. Arizona claimed 66,000 new residents in 2020. Most relocators were leaving the cold North for warmer winter weather. California lost about 176,000 residents fleeing high taxes and high crime cities.[4] Others purchased a second home to try snowbirding to stay relatively warm and comfortable throughout the year, while others-who could be referred to as lizards-purchased for a permanent relocation. They were strong enough to be dry-cured while withstanding the summer heat that hit a record of 120 degrees during the 2020 summer. And in our micro-climate, according to a neighbor, his home weather station recorded 130 degrees in 2023. Other residents are resilient enough to either tolerate or eradicate the armored monstrous insects.

In 2020, we joined the throngs and set our prospects on Mohave County lying between the Black Mountains and the Dead Mountains, east of the Colorado River. The names did not sound promising, yet we zeroed in on Mohave specifically. Why? Because it was one of the closer areas in Arizona to our Washington state northern home, and for the winter season, Mohave has warmer temperatures than in Maricopa County. After all, the purpose was to get away from the dreary cold northern winters. Maricopa County, where our friends own homes, is another five hours beyond or a half day's drive. We were fed up with the drizzly weather in the Pacific Northwest. Fed up with the increasingly noisy streets and the viewpoints that diminished our quality of life.

We began our online research through various realtor websites and learned a lot about the lifestyles of the locals. Many of the listing descriptions wrote "Room for all of your river and desert toys". Storage space seemed to be an important amenity. After viewing hundreds of pictures, in my opinion, it seemed that an addition to that phrase, the words "and room for all of your doll and knick-knack collections" would have been an added bonus. Many of the homes built in the 1990s had vaulted ceilings with pot shelving. These archways or shelves extended out from the walls or served as an archway over connecting open rooms. Owners fully utilized these shelves for displaying panoplies of knick-knacks. There was always a theme-be it airplanes, dolls, hand fans, model cars, or flower vases. If the home had no built-in shelving, either wooden shelves were added or the collections would be lined up on windowsills, on a fireplace mantel, and on top of kitchen cabinets. Another oddity, and reason unknown to me, was close-up pictures of the owner's clothing hanging in walk-in closets. The advertisements did not mention that clothing was for sale. Why would a buyer be interested in seeing each tightly packed closet with polos or t-shirts or tropical shirts in all colors, each hanging on their own individual hangar or double rows of baseball caps on the full length of the shelves? But these were the sellers' oddities that I could look past. We would not decorate nor have the need for a lot of storage space in a rental or a second home.

Another feature that seemed important in the area was an air-conditioned doghouse with artificial turf and a dog run. In motor home communities, the ratio of people with dogs is much higher than in other communities. With 120 plus degree temperatures, our dog would probably appreciate a cool space.

Our internet search took six months. There were hundreds of homes with standard garages for sale but few with the tall garage door needed to house our motor home. The plan was to spend a month in Arizona reviewing neighborhoods and then make our offer. Sometimes plans have to be altered due to circumstances perhaps beyond your control and you need to go with the flow.

Our plan to learn as much as we could over the summer, then head to Arizona for a month to become familiar with the nuances of neighborhoods, and then make an offer was thwarted by a brisk real estate market with competing offers as the norm. During those six months of research, we made two separate offers without the opportunity of visiting.

Over the spring and summer we researched the weather and other pertinent living conditions, read many blogs on "Best Places to Live", scrutinized many photographs, aerials, and real estate agents' listing descriptions. We also had to come to terms with and remember some fun street names, such as, Donkey Drive. Regarding those street names; Sandtrap Way–I stayed clear of that road; Coffee Pot Road–I could get a buzz there; Distant Drums–would I get a headache living on that road? Doodlebug Road–I mean really? Bucket of Blood–ok, how deep into the 'wild west' do I want to be?

We later learned not to let names fool us. For example, RV parks named after rivers or lakes included maps in their brochures showing the park adjacent to water. Reading between the lines, that amenity could refer to a river of highway traffic, or a historical river that is now a dried-up river bed of cobble.

Overall, the statistics and facts, as we read them, convinced us that a desert area was the place for us. All conditions seemed manageable. Warm weather, soft breezes, and clear skies to view the stars. We fantasized about sitting out on a dry patio for alfresco cocktail hours, and having breakfast in the glass surrounded Arizona Room accessed via the bedroom's sliding glass doors. Who could resist that?

Our second offer was accepted. We were so excited and impatient as we headed to our unseen second home, in Arizona, for the winter.

Desert 911

Our route was set and carefully planned. Internet GPS maps indicated that a direct no-stop route would take 20 hours and 30 minutes to travel beginning in central Washington through Oregon and California to reach our final destination in Arizona. We estimated that over a four-day journey, driving 1,300 miles at a leisurely average of 50 miles per hour plus rest stops, our trip would take 26 hours of actual driving.

We packed quite a load, in two vehicles, with basic living necessities to furnish the kitchen and bath. I drove the motor home and Joseph drove his SUV. Following our set route, the first day's seven hours of driving 400 miles went quite smoothly. That night we camped in Grants Pass, Oregon at the Rogue River RV Park. A canopy of tall trees provided some privacy between the narrow sites. Our campsite was a few steps off a slope to the Rogue River. From our camper, there was a clear view down the river to the western setting sun. The swishing sound of the water's ripples was divine and brought soothing whispers to our ears throughout the night.

On our journey, we would travel over two mountain passes. What was not expected, were so many large semi-trucks on the road and the roller coaster highways. The news media had been deceiving in reporting on the lack of truck drivers and the shortage of supplies. During our trip, we saw more supply trucks than passenger vehicles.

We are tourists and at any opportunity we take in some of the sites and scenery along the way by not speeding, and staying within five miles per hour of the speed limit. Anything less than five miles per hour over the speed limit is too slow for truckers. It seemed that the truckers got a kick out of trying to get as close to us as possible. Truckers trying to cover as many miles as possible in a day will pass on the left, test their driving skills by driving over the lane line coming within inches of your driver's side, pass you, and then return to the slow lane less than a cars length in front of you and then for fun, apply their brakes.

There is one situation when truckers do not speed. This timing and speed alteration was not calculated into our estimated time frame. While ascending mountain passes, semi-trucks with heavy loads c-r-a-w-l. Twenty miles per hour at their top speed. Over a four-mile distance, that felt like hours on a one-lane highway. Descending, the bigger rigs use lower gears to slow the vehicle to prevent brake burnout and runaway loss of control and therefore typically do not drive over 40 miles per hour. Evidence of previous vehicles swerving off the roads was indicated by many black tire marks ending in ditches and off the highway. These ribbon patterns did not help our anxiety.

At the slow rate of speed over the mountain pass it was a couple of hours by the time we were able to get a cellular phone signal. Too late to reserve a spot at the last RV park on our list in Barstow, California. By 3:00 p.m. all campsites were full. The next best that we could hope for would be to see signage for another park or rest area along the way.

Cell coverage was spotty or nonexistent in outlying areas. We utilized 2-way radios for communication between our vehicles. They were handy for alerting the following vehicle of dangers ahead, or when one of us needed a rest stop.

This was early November and getting dark by 6 p.m. We knew of no other RV Parks or rest stops en route, so we decided to venture on straight to Arizona and hope that the RV Park, where we had a reservation for the following day, would have a vacancy a day earlier for us.

Onward we drove without boondocking. It was a dark, black night. Except for the large semi-trucks tunneling me in and the occasional reflective lane markers, it was pitch-black. No moon, no street lighting, no signage, no stores nor fueling stations. My tired eyes were straining to see the road. The fuel gauge on the SUV had gone down to the red zone. GPS didn't list any stations ahead.

"Accident debris in the road!" Joseph radioed to warn me, too late. After driving over accident debris which had left wire mesh and metal fragments in the roadway, we stopped at a rest stop to check our tires. Also parked there was the pick-up truck and travel trailer that was driving ahead of us. The driver was also checking his tires and told us the wire mesh had wrapped around an axle, and debris had speared and flattened one of his tires. After we checked our under-carriage, tires, and found all ten tires to be inflated without any fragments embedded, we resumed our route.

As we headed further into civilization and through small towns, the roads opened up and leveled out. We thanked our lucky stars that we drove safely through the Dead Mountains without any mishaps. Quite possibly, we could reach our destination by 9 p.m.

We knew civilization was near seeing billboard after billboard. What a surprise, since this type of advertising was diminished during the "Beautification of America" era during the mid-1960s. In 1965, President Johnson signed the Highway Beautification Act into law which regulated the type and location of advertising billboards on highways. These signs were the tall flag style on a metal pole. Not the more architecturally designed concrete pillars that we see today.

Lights from more vehicles, billboards, and street lighting, helped our tired eyes, as we approached the town of Needles and a fueling station! With less than two gallons to spare, we made it.

Finally, leaving California, we entered onto Highway 95 in Arizona. This stretch of highway is tree-lined, bordering agricultural farms and Indian reservations.

What is that stench? Uff! What an unpleasant odor that we had never smelled before. Skunk? No. But just as pungent. Eucalyptus? No, not so foliage scented. Petroleum? Unknown. Could it have been some oily type residue from a farming equipment accident? The travel and sales brochures never mentioned nor described such an odor! I prayed this would not be a constant rural aroma, as we had acquired a house, sight unseen, as well as never having been to this county before.

After driving 157 miles from Barstow, CA, we arrived at the RV park at 9:30 p.m. The office was closed. Instructions were posted for late arrivals with information on where to park and the rental fee to be paid when the office opens. We were relieved to find one last space available.

Two days later we visited, for the first time, our new home. Wow. Entering the cavernous garage, we wondered if we had gotten into something bigger than what we could handle. After three days on the road, my equilibrium was still compensating for motion. Joseph grabbed my shoulders as I nearly fell backward, looking up to the 18-foot high ceiling.

The house had most everything we desired. Fortuitously it was located in a newer neighborhood that we had previously considered four years ago; however, at that time we did not pursue the dream of snowbirding. The development is still under construction and is being built slowly. One neighborhood will consist of humungous garages with a small one-bedroom and living area at the rear of the building. Did I forget to mention that this is an RV haven? Some garages are over 55-feet long and have room for five standard vehicles.

We had dreamed and planned on a new custom home; however, the wait time to completion would have taken a bare minimum of 10 months, with 15 months being more typical. As luck would have it, a two-year-old resale became available in one of the newer developments. There were some missing wanna-haves and compromises in the property. My dream of a cacti xeri-scape garden was in reality a lush tree-lined perimeter garden with several fruit trees, flowering shrubs, and water-hungry palms. Joseph was happy, as he had always wanted at least one fruit tree and the palms reminded him of many vacations taken on tropical islands. In my viewpoint the palms resembled monster feather dusters on a long slender post. I was slightly intrigued with the garden because I love variety in year-round colors, the hummingbirds that visit, and the scents that flowers emit. However, I do not appreciate the work.

Our hope for a small house and a two-car garage sufficient to house one small motor home was in reality a comfortable 1,350 square foot home plus an enclosed 200 square foot porch, an attached 1,150 square foot garage and a detached 290 square foot shed that could house a vehicle or our newly anticipated tiki bar room. Interior parking for five to six cars, boats or big man toys, and exterior on-site parking for seven or more vehicles. Well, we can live with that!

In our planning stages, we dreamt that we would design a custom home in a planned development with shared amenities such as: a swimming pool, community hall, private restaurant, and a golf course. In reality, this newer development had no shared amenities, lacked the hundreds of dollars in homeowner dues, and was at the outskirts of town. We were at the edge of a desert.

It is so quiet. Eerily quiet. The very first morning I woke early and did not hear the familiar sounds of traffic, no barking dogs, no rumbling of jets overhead. Slowly I opened my eyes, at first confused by my surroundings and then it dawned on me. I am in Arizona.

After a few weeks, we adjusted to our new surroundings and translated our dream into the new reality.

* * *

Edge of the desert. We came for the silence. The atmosphere can be so calm, dead still, without sound, and no leaves rustling. One can almost hear the scorpions and fire ants making trails through the sand. As well as the horny nails of lizards scratching the concrete driveway as they scamper to find refuge in the mini-split air conditioner.

What was I thinking? Due to the proximity to the desert, we did not realize that most owners also have All Terrain Vehicles (ATVs). This is serious business. (Translation: work). At least three times per week and on schedule at nine in the morning, drivers roar out to roam the desert, on the other side of our fence, for unknown reasons. By four o'clock, they roar back and party. Beers on the house!

Edge of the desert. We came to get away from the gray, wet and moldy northwest. A desert is classified as having 10 inches or less of rain per year. My online pre-investigations on weather sites reported an average of six inches of rain per year and low humidity which would dry out aching bones and relieve asthma.

What was I thinking? The pocket microclimate area we are in has about four inches of rain per year. I wondered if there's another classification for that. Even cacti dry and shrivel up. With minimal humidity sometimes as low as four percent, plants can barely draw moisture from the air.

We had been here for two weeks when there were clouds one afternoon. "Look Joseph. It is raining."

"What? I don't see anything."

This was a photo opportunity. "It has been raining for 15 minutes. Look up!"

"They call this rain? Most of the drops dry up before reaching the concrete."

"The weather reports indicated 'Not measurable'. Even so, I didn't expect this much moisture. But, let's call it what it is! This weather effect is called virga." [5]

Was there any rainfall? Yes, we can now turn on the faucet. The Water Conservation District has asked everyone to conserve water due to the record heat of 120 degrees and severe dry spell this year.

After any hot day above 85 degrees, one would think that the water in the house pipes would be warm, but NOOOO, the water is ice cold. In the winter mornings, after 30-degree nighttime temperatures, the opposite occurs. The water is warm.

Did I mention DRY? There is a reason that the supermarket shelves are lined with flavored water drinks. Yes, the desert is dry and that means lathering lots of oil on my skin. Otherwise, lizard skin. Oh, my neighbors look SO OLD! Hats or shade cloths provide little relief, as the concrete will reflect heat and bright sun to burn your skin. Indeed, the skies are bright without cloud cover and the air so dry that your eyes may turn into prunes.

Edge of the desert. We came for a rock, crystal, and cacti low-maintenance landscape. I was looking forward to growing a natural xeri-scape garden with lots of cacti, including saguaros, ocotillos, and succulents.

What was I thinking? In reality, my low-maintenance dream cacti garden was not. That is true. In reality, a lush tree-lined perimeter garden was planted by the previous owners with several bottle brushes (*Callistemon viminalis*), six outstanding Orange Jubilees (*Tecoma alata*), five willows (*Acacia stenophylla*), three citrus trees, and three Indian Rosewoods (*Dalbergia sissoo*). The Rosewoods sport small delicate leaves, and in the spring produce the tiniest bundle of sweet fragrant white flowers. Several flowering shrubs; including five Mexican petunias (*Ruellia simplex*), a desert Bird of Paradise (*Caesalpinia gilliesii*), six Texas sages (*Leucophyllum frutescens*), and four water-hungry palms that remain scientifically unidentified.

Ready to start a garden section with cacti, we planted 10 starts of prickly pear and chollas. Fifteen days later we walked the garden to review our relandscaping plan.

"Honey, where are and how many cacti did we plant?"

"We planted 10 in the raised bed and one cholla in the corner. So, why did you plant one within the orange tree canopy?"

"I didn't! And look closely, a large bite is on the side." Unbelievable.

Any cacti located near water that were plump and didn't dry up were eaten by our resident Antelope squirrels. A big name for a squirrel that is the size of a chipmunk. Our 'adopted pets' ended my dream for a cacti garden.

Our plants are fed by a timed irrigation system. More water results in more growth. Less water results in dying brown sticks. We have not found a happy medium. The watered plants grow so fast that growth can be seen on some plants from day to day. Over the winter, we have pruned the trees every month. Even so, six months later the plants are taller, the branches thicker and the foliage bushier than when we arrived. Seven months of hot summer weather without pruning put another four to five feet of new growth on some of the plants. To avoid heatstroke and death to trees, pruning stops in March. Landscapers advised that due to the extreme hot temperatures and dryness in the summer, any plants pruned in the summer or late spring will die. Perhaps that might be better. We could try that.

With such little annual rainfall, what does that mean for our fruit trees? Fruit trees in the desert? Yes, Arizona is actually known for growing citrus, although mostly at higher elevations like in Sedona and Tucson. We are below 1,000 feet. The sellers left us with two dead fruit trees, one good grapefruit tree, and a half-dead orange tree that is putting out new shoots lower on the trunk. What were they thinking? Most landscapes have native trees on the south side of the home to provide shade. The previous owners planted fruit trees on the south side that will grow to about seven feet, providing no shade for the house, nor the yard.

My gardening neighbor told me that he saw a tree split in half due to a lack of humidity and extensive heat. He advised to install an open weave sun shade to reduce sunburn on sensitive leaves.

There are few plants that can survive in this climate. In the undeveloped open areas around us, there are no native desert shrubs over two feet high. Anything higher or without a taproot and deep feeder roots will be blown over.

Edge of the desert. It is true that dry heat feels about ten degrees cooler than what the outdoor thermometer reads. I had researched that the average wind speed was about 11 to 15 miles per hour. AAAHHH, the ooh-la-la breezes will cool us off out on the patio.

What was I thinking? Views from our home are open and to the horizon. There is nothing to stop the wind, which rips through the valley. Sometimes bringing that desert odor of the creosote plant (*Larrea tridentata*) combined with a wet concrete odor. Most likely that same unwelcoming odor we experienced on our first night drive into town.

We were in the middle of having lunch on the patio surrounded by our oasis in the desert when suddenly a big gust of wind sailed around the corner of the house. With the wind comes the sand from the desert. Blowing sand everywhere. There will be a mouthful of sand in your meal, and grit in your eyes. Solid chairs turned into shallow sand trays. So you have learned your lesson and now eat indoors. But what if you happen to venture outside on a windy day?

The almost constant breezes are punctuated by 40-plus mile-per-hour gusts. In the winter, the colder winds are from the north, and in the summer the hot winds are from the even hotter south. Our house sits in the center of all the winds. The winds circle around the house like a tornado blowing in all directions. Forget what the weather report is. Add about five miles per hour or more for our immediate area. Most of our neighbors have weather stations to rely upon.

Our house is on a corner with a flagpole at the street corner of our property. The ball shaped finial spun off from the force of the storm. We were able to retrieve it lodged between thick plant stems in the front patio.

Winds so strong they leave destruction behind. On a corner, a McDonald's Golden Arches structure was blown down at its base. It lay flat, horizontally, yet did not touch the ground. A brand-new car was crushed. Split right down the middle.[6]

Do you think that a nice sunscreen will protect plants and you from the sun and reduce wind speed? Think again. Yes, we put one up. The screen was ripped apart, and blown away along with my hat. Closely weaved or 60 percent plus shade cloths become a sail and will blow away. We replaced the shade cloth with a 40 percent weave which is holding up much better having less resistance to the wind.

Perhaps you have tied your taller plants down with stakes. Ha! A high-wind storm occurred in January 2021. All of our trees are held in place with at least two one-eighth inch steel cables. One of the steel cables snapped in a 53 mile per hour gust and blew an acacia over. Other stakes were either loosened or pulled out of the ground.

Storm chasers do love this area. Eventually, a strong haboob will develop without warning. Perhaps some of my neighbors could take advantage and use the dust storm as a dermabrasion skin rejuvenation treatment. Should you also venture outdoors to experience the exhilaration of storm watching, you will later find sand and tiny bits of gravel in your naval and in your socks. Leather boots are a necessity to protect your feet from the debris that will find its way through canvas or the top side of your shoe. If it happens to rain real wet rain drops during a haboob, good luck. You will experience a mud storm.

Something that you will not know until you have been here a while are some of the effects of the *wind*. Desert sand does not stay in the desert. You may need to vacuum every night. The sand will infiltrate through window screens and any gaps between the doorframe and the aluminum door, which has been warped by the extreme heat and pressure from winds. Cleaning services will not use a vacuum because the filters quickly clog. I may need to dust every night. This translates into more work for me.

Heavy gusts cause the air pressure in sewer pipes to fall which then can cause the toilet bowl water to dip and rise substantially. A reverse mini tsunami. If your feet weren't solid on the ground, you might believe there was an earthquake.

The winds are not an occasional happenstance. Power interruptions to electrical service and the internet are frequent. Those who have gas are fortunate and may have a generator for power backup.

These are the stories that won't be shown nor read about in national news because the individual incidents are few and scattered throughout the Valley. Not mass destruction to make a note on national news. Yet wind damage is common. You are more likely to read about these occurrences in The Valley News, a local newspaper or the KDMiner out of Kingman. For example: the house that spun in a dust storm. February

21, 2022[7] a dust devil picked up portions of a house, spinning debris everywhere.

Edge of the desert. We also came for astronomy. There will be many nights of clear sky observations. With several cities earning the coveted International Dark Sky designation, a variety of venues would be available most of the year.

What was I thinking? The wind does not stop at night. Dust will be blown into the optics, and the heavier gusts will cause a wiggle even to a 45-pound telescope on a tripod. Even on nights with minimal air movement, the fast cooling of the night air and rising heat from the ground bring air eddies to distort the atmospheric seeing. We are learning to chart the best days for viewing by watching the weather forecast for high-pressure systems that bring clear skies.

Edge of the desert. I was warned about an astrological sign, Scorpio. We got this right and we were ready for them. Armed with a black light that differentiates a Scorpion from a pseudoscorpion. Under a black light, the Scorpion will fluoresce. But that is not all on the edge of the desert.

The insect version of a skunk is the Darkling black bug. Why some people keep these stinkers as pets is beyond me. Ugly, long legged, with smooth black wings that do not function for flying but are used as armor. They will raise their back end up and spray an offensive odor that is difficult to remove. We identified this odor as one noted on our first night driving into town. Their needle-like feet barely come in contact with the ground protecting them from pesticides. The only glee I get out of seeing them is when the wind tosses them, lying on their backs with legs flailing. Moreover, I am not kidding you, these beetles are supersized. Killing these monsters has lost its luster and probably put a hole in the sole of my shoe.

Insects are attracted to moisture and seem to detect extra moisture coming from the exterior faucets and cooking vapors from the roof vents. Crickets manage to jump onto the roof, migrate through vent ducts and fall into the toilet bowls below the ceiling exhaust fans. Should I use an umbrella for the night trips to the bathroom? We could use some snakes to help. Other than lizards, we have not seen any snakes. Yet.

Edge of the desert. In a no-crime area, we will be able to safely walk under the cool night sky.

What was I thinking? Beware of the active, wild nightlife; such as: snakes, Mojave spotted cats, coyotes, and foxes (*Urocyon Cinereoargeoteus*) that roam freely. This fox has sharp, hooked claws that allow them to climb walls and trees. I would not care to come across one. All of these animals and more roam the desert at night. Occasionally, animal howling sounds will penetrate our stucco walls. No one walks here after dark. Bicyclists and walkers get their exercise during the cool hours in the early morning. We found the best times for sitting out are in the early morning, before sunrise, and at twilight to a few hours after sunset. One late evening we were sitting on the back patio and heard low guttural howling. My eyes opened wide, "Did you hear those cries? Sounds like cats mating." We dared not look, lest one jump over the wall. I would love to see what is out there but I am not willing to take on and interfere with a mating ritual that I cannot compete with. Perhaps one day I will roam the desert in an ATV sporting night vision goggles. Then I can surely say with confidence that I am an Arizonian.

Edge of the desert. There will be hummingbirds and flowers year-round. Oh! Yeah! This is true. I was thinking correctly on this topic. Bottlebrush shrubs are about eight to ten feet in height and plush with more red flowering color than green foliage. Bees, sphinx moths, and hummingbirds adore dining on them. Vivid red flowers bloom from March to December with a full flush in April. Hummingbirds sit in the Orange Jubilees, which I have allowed to grow to eleven feet tall. Their tubular flowers provide nectar for the hummingbirds year-round. Sphinx moths are hard to track as they zoom from one Texas sage to the other. The shutter speed on our cameras were too slow to get a still shot of the moths even as they hovered on a flower. We enjoyed the show and counted about twelve moths on one bottlebrush shrub.

This area is a valley, with mountains on the east and west, yet the sunrises and sunsets are quite visible and spectacular in color, and clouds appear as streams. The sky was particularly magnificent on the night of March 28, 2022. Huge cumulus clouds in the east hung over a lower layer of dark gray rain clouds. Towards the west, the darkest gray clouds provided a backdrop to the spectacular silhouette of the Dead Mountain craggy peaks.

Views are open and to the horizon in the south. I feel pure joy walking the sands during the day while I hunt for unusual rocks and shiny crystals. Is this a desert thing? After a few months we believe so, and consider ourselves Arizonites, as interest in the composition of rocks, rock hunting, and collecting has become a hobby. We may need a pot shelf to display our growing collection of quartz, orthoclase, apatite, granite, and other crystals.

If we walk long enough on this sandy desert, we dream that eventually we will arrive at a sandy beach on the Pacific Ocean. Often, we sit on the concrete block wall facing the desert and look beyond to see shimmering waves. These are the liquid mirages of the ocean in our minds. We are mesmerized by the crystals and sand. And when there is some rain, the resulting odors do resemble those of ocean beaches.

Edge of the desert. Yeah, you can visualize all of the resort-type advertising that beckons relocators and travelers to Arizona. But in the end, it is still the edge of the desert. A mirage.

On the way back

Our vehicle was covered in dust and bug splotch. With a severe drought plaguing the area, we decided to conserve water and not wash our vehicle. Dust had blown through cracks in the doorframe and had settled and accumulated on our vehicles which were parked in the garage. In an attempt to dislodge the particles, we drove at a high rate of speed on the highway. The speed was fun and exhilarating, but did little to remove the sand. The dust and sand layers still adhered and functioned as a sandblaster scouring the surface of the hood.

We considered using the automated drive through car wash, but passed it by when we saw grackles waiting on the roof, flying through water clouds and jumping in pools of water on the ground.

How do locals keep their cars so bright and shiny? With the exception of work trucks, personal vehicles all seemed clean and shiny. This amazed us. We should have paid more attention to the local weather reports. The weather announcer actually reported on the best weather days for washing a car. The 'Car Report' was to wash before the rains that were expected that week. The City of Mesa has a brochure listing tips for car washing. [8]

Although water is in scarce supply, there is a whole lot of washing going on. My neighbors wash the dust off their ATVs after each joy ride in the desert. Seems like a lot of work. My schedule for that washing task is one hour per year, if that; and to be accomplished while it is raining, to make the job easier for myself. A good rain in Washington will help remove grime.

"We'll be in Washington soon. Four more days and our cars will be clean."

Traveling through California, it is clear that farmers have been exasperated with drought conditions and Congress's handling of the water and agricultural crises. Several signs along the I-5 and Highway 99 corridors scream the messages– "No Water, No Food" or "We Use Water to Grow Food", "Farmers Feed America", and "Food Grows Where Water Flows". One farm with a water tower near the highway depicted Uncle Sam holding a bunch of grapes with the words-"The Magic of Water". Several dead orchards revealed the consequences of lack of water.[9] And another message to politicians-"Don't Drain our Water to The Ocean".[10]

We were thankful for the light rain as we drove for 15 miles through Sutherlin, Oregon. While the rain cleared some of the dust off, it did nothing better for the bug carcasses but to spread them out.

Back in Washington after only two days I lament, "Damp. Cold. Oh, I miss the dry earth and warmth of the air."

Joseph dreamily states, "Crystals are calling. I have plans to search a new area for copper and those little black pebbles you called Apache Tears."

Would we make the trek again?

You betcha!

Mesmerized *

"You have bewitched me, body and soul"
Pride and Prejudice (2005)

Is it my imagination or is there something about the combination of constant sun and dry heat in Arizona that puts residents into a stupor? Let's delve into a few behaviors that I have witnessed.

Activity #1:

The public library opens at 11:00 a.m. Not knowing that, as a new resident, I arrived at 10:45 a.m. I saw the CLOSED sign clearly posted on the door and waited in the car. For the next 14 minutes, at least six locals got out of their cars, walked to the door with the big CLOSED sign with listed hours of operation and they each tried pulling the door. Not once, but several times. The locked door did not open on its own, nor by their efforts.

What were they thinking? That an employee might have left the door unlocked? Opened early? Might they have come from another time zone?

Activity #2

Shopping for food is not a social activity. I go into a supermarket knowing what is needed and waste no time grabbing items from the shelves with a short pause to check the pull date on packages and reject any dented cans or broken packages. I zoom past other shoppers and if their cart is in the way, it is soon not. Good luck locating your cart fellow shopper. Yes, I am a speed shopper; no one gets in my way.

If you are ever in Mohave, take note of the shopping habits of the locals. In particular, walk through the bloody meat section. This aisle is twice the width of other aisles. Shopping for meat could be a mind-altering experience. A coming to the Hereford's or Red Devon's grassy gates, which would translate as the pearly gates for humans. The locals will mill around the meat section as if in a trance. What might they be waiting for? When they aren't milling, their heads are bent down staring at the meat as if they were searching for written instructions on what their next move should be. One ~~zombie~~, oh excuse me, I meant woman. One woman was staring wide-eyed at the packaged beef, head bent down, and body leaning forward. After a few minutes, she stroked a package, gently picked it up, and ever so slowly and reverently slid the packaged beef into a plastic bag, all the while caressing the package.

The meat is freshly butchered and I will admit that the quality of the beef is outstanding. Yet, I wonder, what are they waiting for? What are they thinking? Will they have a revelation?!!

Activity #3:

Most neighborhoods are fairly quiet and residents keep to themselves. Perhaps in some cases too much. At least three times per week, one fellow in our neighborhood takes a short walk to the end of his driveway and stands at the curb for a few minutes. He will look to the east down the street, look to the west down the street. Again. Left, right. Repeating this several times. What is he looking for? Is he waiting for a ride? I have not figured it out. I have observed hummingbirds perform this exact behavior while standing watch over their territory.

Occasionally this same fellow will break his left-right routine and will stand in the street and spin slowly. Pivoting in one place while looking up at the clear sky. I question if he is spinning within himself or if he is trying to make a connection with the solar system that is spinning around him. I have some theories and believe that I have figured out that performance. Perhaps he was affected by a UFO. Or perhaps the location provides a psychedelic vibe from a strong vortex. It is said that in Arizona there are supernatural vortexes and magical crystals in the desert. Many people have experienced the pull of spiritual energy from the rocks and natural formations in an Arizona desert. Thoughts and feelings are amplified in the region.

After a few months of observing this behavior, I believe the vortex theory has been substantiated. Greater roadrunners inhabit this area and run in straight lines along the top of concrete walls and on the ground. One day, a roadrunner ran through a few front yards and came to a stop on this neighbor's front driveway. He ran in a small circle, stopped, and then circled in the opposite direction. He stopped, looked west, looked east, and then turned north to run to the owner's backyard. Movements that were very similar to the movements of the property owner. There has to be a vortex around that driveway.

Our valley is an inflow site that is conducive to introspection and contemplation. A definite stress reducer. If rain clouds return bringing rain and moisture, I'll look to the heavens to be washed and I will begin to grow again.

The most beautiful sunsets.

Activity #4 that you may witness:

On clear mornings and evenings, I gaze upon an open valley spanning a southern 200-degree view over miles of desert. In the morning, looking to the left, the sunrise greets me. A light pink line of light over the Black Hills is followed by an orange glow. Wispy white clouds all foretell another beautiful clear and sunny day.

In the evening, the sun bids adieu. I look to the right. Blazing fire-red and orange hues above a light golden sheen, the sun sets behind the Dead Mountain Wilderness Area in California. In contrast, darker gray streaked cirrus clouds form wispy long contrails like a horse's tail.

I watch the movement of the sun and I am mesmerized.

One day, someone may observe me, sitting on our concrete block wall facing south throughout the day. Beneath my feet crystals and minerals shimmer as I sight on the sun following its path from early morning til sunset. At that point, I can say I am mesmerized and have truly melted into the Arizona experience.

Route 66

Our good friends drove 1,300 miles to become parched, desiccated, and nauseated in an Arizonan desert. They made their first trek in January 2022 to visit us. They arrived in their 19-foot Road Trek Class B motorhome and hooked up on our RV pad, between the desert and our garage.

The Mohave area of Arizona was new to us also and we were geared up to see the sites and show our guests how wonderful the desert is.

Arizona is an 'open range' state. Livestock and wildlife cross roads even in our built-up valley town which is sandwiched between the Black Mountains on the east and the Colorado River on the west. Snakes, jackrabbits, coyotes, foxes, and Mohave Desert Cats have been seen transiting and hunting in our neighborhood of single-story homes.

One wild animal we have not seen are camels. [11] In the mid-1850s, 77 camels were brought into Arizona by the United States government for use as pack animals for the miners. The animals did not fare well. Their feet have webbing between the toes and as such were not suited for rocks and cacti spines. Even without camels, there are a sufficient number of wild animals to avoid while driving. Burros roam freely in the town of Oatman and have been crossing Bullhead Parkway in Bullhead City.

We decided to treat Laurie and Rusty to the most exciting section of the 'Mother Road' (National Trails Highway). A nine-mile-long section that is considered one of the riskiest, most exhilarating to drive as compared to other treacherous roads. Driving, watching the road, and taking in the spectacular views-"Watch out!" are real tests of your multi-tasking abilities.

Beware the signs that state "No Vehicles Over 14 Feet Long", or "Steep Grade", or "Sharp Curves Next 4 miles". These are understatements. Our comfortable 2009 Toyota ForeRunner, with 4-wheel drive, was well short of the stated vehicular length. There would be no issue in navigating curves and steep slopes.

Guard rails are nonexistent. The road varies in width and can be generous at about 16 feet wide with steep drop-offs on the north side, and cliffs on the southerly side. There are some soft shoulders where you can pull over to rest, take pictures or allow other vehicles to pass. Hard shoulders exist also, but not for a safe stop. These hard 'shoulders' can be unstable rocks, a shrugged cliff or a poured concrete four-inch curb on the edge that is sloughing down.

I was comfortable with Joseph driving as he is aware of his surroundings and is a skillful driver. Our passengers in the back were not as confident.

As we drove along, Rusty and I took in the scenery. A couple of dirt roads in the deep canyons on the left led to a house or two and also to quarries and mines. In the far distance we spotted a narrow dirt road that led to a small house. We wondered what it would be like to live there and if the property had utilities and power. I found out later the home is owned by a fellow who lives off the grid and is an avid protector of the wild burros.

The sheer nakedness of the terrain is sheathed in color. Stratified layers of adularia in whites and grays, crystal white quartz, faded greens of chlorite, white streaks in calcite, brassy yellows of pyrite...

Laurie suddenly squealed, "Oh there is a sharp curve coming up. Joseph, please slow down." Which he did, resulting in less sway and side motion.

We passed a gold mine[12]; a cemetery; Sitgreaves Pass at 3,595 feet is the highest point; Cuesta Fire Agate Mine, and three memorial sites--a forewarning to drive defensively and skillfully.

As Laurie slid lower in her seat, her voice quivered, "Oh, I think I'm getting a bit disoriented. There are so many turns."

I opened a window in preparation for a possible up-chuck. "Lay low; we will be at our destination in a few minutes."

By the time we reached Cool Springs, after 10 miles on the route, Laurie appeared nauseated and both of our guests were ready for a walk to calm their dizzy heads and catch their breath. Near the edge of a cliff is Cool Springs Station. It was once a gas station and is now a souvenir shop. The view overlooks Golden Valley canyon and the Hualapai mountain range at a distance of only about 30 air miles. Hualapai Peak was clearly viewable to the east at over 8,300 feet shadowing granite pillars.

After our respite, Laurie was able to appreciate the views and she marveled at the strata layers across the canyons. "The colors are magnificent. Do you think we can prospect for copper?"

"Arizona may be known as the Copper State, but I don't recommend chiseling away in this heat."

During the 1860s gold mining was the draw for thousands of prospectors. Today, the population is sparse and only a few hundred mining activities in the county remain active.

Sign at Cool Springs

Off-roading is a popular activity in the desert and most true Arizonians have an All-Terrain Vehicle (ATV). Especially if you need to cut across the desert to get to another town or just to have a drink in isolation.

Rusty wanted a bit more authentic experience, as he had heard stories of the wide open region attracting hikers and off-roaders. Fortuitously he was invited by other friends to explore and rock crawl the desert in an ATV. He thought he was ready. I watched him pack a meager supply kit. Water bottle-check; extra jacket-check; hat with visor-check; goggles-check.

"Are you not taking equipment? When we go out we are sure to bring a cross-bow, machete, first-aid kit...

"No, I think I'll be okay," he interrupted as he looked at me with a questioning expression.

"At the very least bring a small ax. The vehicle does not have a roll cage. You may have to hack your way out of a prickly pear bed."

His eyebrows and eyes scrunched, giving me a sideways crazy look. Okay, enough advice to Mr. Mountaineer, who had taught wilderness safety classes in the wet and forested Northwest and was proficient in propelling. He did not want to hear another word. He waved good-bye and purposefully exited the house.

About six hours later, Rusty shakily walks in, quickly heading directly to the sink with his 24-ounce water bottle in hand. Hair standing out, face parched with dust, not saying a word.

"Well. How was the outing?" I grinned anxious to hear about any possible confrontation with wildlife or spiny plant.

"Oh, it was good. We took it easy and stopped at overlooks. We came across two other off-roaders." Rehydrated, and trying to look cool, he sat down, shook sand out of his sneakers, pulled out his phone, and we went through his pictures of fields of flowers, animal dens, and views of canyons.

"It was amazing to see so many flowers in soil that appears so arid. And I didn't need no stinking machete!"

They enjoyed the area so much they stayed for three and a half weeks.

10 *The Silver Years*

During my sixties, I took pleasure in a true change of lifestyle-retirement! Finally, retirement arrived to do more or less of what I chose to do. A time for more dreaming and living the life I learned and grew into.

Drilled into my head from the time I was a teenager, my father would say, "Stay in your government job. In 30 years, you can retire by the time you are 50. Then you can work on any of the hobbies you care to."

He always mentioned retirement and he himself retired at 52 years of age to relocate to Florida and start his own full-time plumbing business. He truly enjoyed working outdoors and considered it his playtime. Because of those examples from his life, I learned to always mention retirement and dreamt of consulting work to keep busy after retirement. My consulting play/work became a hobby in giving presentations to garden clubs and editing newsletters. Unfortunately, having started late in my government jobs, I waited until I was 60 to retire. Had I to do it over, retirement would have come at least two years sooner.

Age of Electronics *

Being newly retired in the Millennial decade puts me in the category of the over-60 crowd growing up during the influential '60s love generation era. A touchy-feely person. I like the feel of a key or a pen, or even a book in my hand.

I mean, I am not implying computer illiteracy. Starting in the 1980s and continuing 32 years later in past vocations, I have adapted to the many changes in computer programs. Earlier systems ran on Command Line DOS (Disc Operating System) which made sense. Data stroke input, visual equivalent output. Later, computer systems advanced to using Windows for charts and formulas. Even though calculations seemed automatic and might have been relied upon, I had been taught to think and found some of the completed calculations to be wrong. By recalculating in my head, or on paper, I did indeed find inaccuracies.

Now in an emoji era of what seems like magic, a wand or a finger swipe is used on a device the size of a compact makeup case. The print is too small or menus are hidden and one needs to click twice or thrice for an outcome that previously was either immediately available or required only a single click. The newer programs do not make sense. Input does not equate to output.

What has happened to "user-friendly"? All of a sudden without my approval, "Big Step-brother" decided to have my saved documents open in a browser! I am outraged, put beside myself wondering, "What the heck happened?" "Big Step-brother" calls it an "upgrade". I call it a wasteful-grade. Now when opening a document there are extra steps to make-click on 'open with', change the program and click. Sure, that's only two extra clicks, but taken hundreds of times each day results in too much wasted idle time when the time could have been spent on meaningful writing or doing.

Eventually, I'll figure it out. Some short-cut or perhaps using a different vendor. In my lifetime there will still be choices and ingenuity.

Look at the car industry. My trusty 14-year-old Subaru Forester began to cost over 1,000 dollars each year in replacement parts and service charges. In 2012, I visited a few dealerships. Wow. I experienced amenity and operation shock. I did not expect vehicular changes to advance to the age of being computer driven and accessed without a key in hand. The first look at a 2012 no-key entry Toyota sent me running from the dealership.

By 2014, I could no longer postpone replacing my vehicle. The search was on for a new vehicle. I started by noting any interesting new cars on the roadways. A hot sleek car on the highway caught my eye. Time to update my criteria for choosing vehicles. Fast, smooth lines, and low. Previously the solid styling and size of a Subaru Forester caught my eye in 1998 and I knew then that was the car for me. This new update to my selection criteria could work.

To the dealership, I drove. The car was impressive during the test drive and I was comfortable with the no-pressure salesperson. Within two hours a signature on the dotted line was completed. Somehow, I had totally overcome my aversion to a no-touch, no-entry key, high-tech mode of transportation.

An announcement in 2016 from Tesla's Elon Musk stated that soon, self-driving vehicles will operate without any input from the driver. Ford would have self-driving vehicles in 2021 and GMC will produce cars without a steering wheel or other manual control. What is a driver to do? Autonomous driving must be why Atari games are displayed on the dash. Sleep or play and go. Sounds good to me. Welcome to the Age of Electronics.

Age of Electronics part 2

Labor-saving devices became common in many households during the 1950s. Appliances such as; the automatic dishwasher, clothes washers and drying machines, electric vacuum cleaners, and phone answering machines. Appliances were like the plug-and-play toys of the 1990s, but the labor-saving devices were for adults.

Engineers of the day invented easy to use appliances. Simply plug a cord into a wall socket, press a start button, and the machine took care of the rest.

Recently in 2020, I had to make the unfortunate purchase of a new electronic washing machine to replace a 22-year-old plug and play machine. In this newer era, appliances are technologically advanced with added program features that the manufacturers claim will lighten your labor. Numerous variable features can be selected and many choices have to be made to match the size, weight, and type of fabric to be washed. Length of time, temperature, steam dry, and a delay feature are other options. The manual is 40 pages long.

Is this a time-saving apparatus? Time to read the manual takes about 40 minutes, five minutes to sort the clothing, two minutes to decide on which option to push, select not one but up to four options, and then hold the start for four seconds. TOO MUCH WORK! TOO MUCH IDLE TIME! Excuse me; I have to run to the kitchen to cook...

The manual contains a few important caveats. If not read, the machine will clank loudly if the clothing was not distributed properly and eat your socks. Several socks have taken a hike this week. Do you think it's obvious where to add detergent? There are three receptacles. One of which will take powder or liquid depending upon the position of the inlet door. If you did not read the manual, you are likely to add a liquid detergent into the powder-only receptacle. Raised white lettering on a white background is not easily read. The lettering can barely be seen from a break-neck angle and by using a bright light source.

Where are the machines that have two buttons or two dials? Throw the clothing in, add soap, turn the knob to ON and let the machine do the work.

None of these modern advanced features match my style of washing clothing. I prefer plug-and-play.

Another unfortunate purchase was the replacement of my cell phone for 5G capability. My "old" 15-year-old reliable 3G phone still had a two-week battery life before it needed to be recharged, but coverage was becoming spotty.

Coverage is slightly better with 5G, but the battery life is much shorter at only ten days. The old three-click process of opening my contact list, selecting a name and pressing send has turned into a frustrating maze. A few menus have been added. Five clicks to get the contact page, three clicks to see a list of contacts, another click or scroll to the contact name and hit send? No. Not an option. Another click for the method of sending and another to send. Counting eleven or more clicks. It is faster to recall a number by memory and dial it outright. A test and practice on memorization are beneficial exercises.

Telephone exchanges were phased out in the 1960s. In New York our exchange was TWining – so the phone number was 89#####. It was a notable system and facilitated recall.

With today's cell phones, talk fast because the connection can fail at any time.

And warranty? Forget it. In another few years I imagine this phone call will be made:

"Hello, is this customer service? I am calling to find out about the warranty on my cell phone that died."

"When did you purchase the phone and do you have a receipt?"

"I purchased the phone six months ago and yes; I have the receipt."

"What can I help you with?"

"I understand that this model has a lifetime warranty. One of the keys failed and the battery died yesterday."

"Yes, ma'am. There is a warranty for the life of the battery and a one-year for the unit. But that model has no manufacturer defects and since the battery died, the life is over. The warranty is terminated and no longer applies. As for the key failure, it has to be from overuse, which is not covered."

I now prefer my landline with extremely clear reception and without dropped calls.

Which do you prefer?

Electromagnetism

It is said that opposites attract. My husband is the negative and I am the positive. He is the North and I am the South. Psychologists dispute this human polarity and say the concept applies to the science world in electromagnetic valence and charges. Human relationships, they say, are more stable when personalities, style, and beliefs are similar

Our relationship seems to be an exception, as we play off of one another; our polarity is probably why our marriage has lasted 40 years.

I have a habit of bending and crunching anything in my hands. Forget access to a hotel room. The key card is a lost cause. In order to enable access to a hotel room, my husband has to take charge of the key card to prevent destruction of the card and to keep the coded connection secure. When I attempt to insert a card, even one that is new and straight, the electronics become disabled. This is most likely due to my strong magnetism.

As we furnished our new home, in the 1980s, our discussion turned to television sets. "I really like my black and white portable TV. The picture is clear and it doesn't hurt my eyes like color does."

"But there is no remote," Joseph argued.

"So, what. The television works and so do our legs. We can get up from the couch to change the channel. It's good exercise."

We didn't have to argue for long, as reception was practically nonexistent in the neighborhood and we had to install cable.

But here is the problem. Computers and remote television controls don't always respond to my touch, regardless of whether there is a button or a touch screen. Our older remote had buttons. On rare occasions, the toggle switch will function for me. What I long for are good old knobs. When television channels won't change after I repeatedly push a selection, my husband in frustration will grab the remote. Then I'll hear, "Move out of the line of fire." With one press on the button, he has changed the channel - unless I didn't get out of the target area in time. Then the remote might not work.

A similar problem occurs with microwave ovens. Our modern oven, manufactured in 2017, has touch 'sensitive' selectors. You would think this is a simple operation. I have used the pad of my finger tip, a finger nail tap, I have pressed hard, pressed lightly. Regardless of the technique I have used, a few attempts are required before the microwave will respond. Or a starving husband will use his one touch magic finger.

Okay, this isn't funny. I am usually hungry and impatient in the kitchen. The new electromagnetic induction cooking range heats rapidly. That is why I bought it. No fuss, no waiting. Turn a knob on and the magnetic pots heat up in an instant. Boiling water takes about five seconds to reach an appropriate boiling point.

So, here I am ready with pot on the stovetop, food in the pot. I turn the dial... No light. Each dial is surrounded by a light indicating the burner is turned on. Okay, retry. Turn the dial off. Turn the dial on. No light. Burner not heating. Third and final try: Still the same result. Electronic Man Joseph who can fix computers by standing next to them is summoned.

"Honey! Would you help with the cooking?" I was not about to admit I did not know how to operate a Wi-Fi enabled cook-top. And I was too hungry to spend time reading the lengthy manual. Mr. Electronic Man with magic fingers arrives and turns the dial. Lo and behold the indicator light turns on and the burner becomes hot.

Who would have guessed? Ha!

It has to be my electromagnetism causing an energy wave disrupting communication. If brain-machine interface devices become commonplace within my lifetime, I might malfunction and will have to opt out.

On most shopping excursions the self-checkout in supermarkets has been a great convenience for me to speed through stores. I knew how to operate one. One day, I brought my own bags, tapped start, scanned the first item and the machine stopped working. The checker came over to restart it and nothing happened. After a few frustrating attempts she became flustered, "I don't know why this is happening. I will help you at another register to get you checked out."

On another shopping spree, I had placed half of my groceries on the conveyor belt. Leaning over to give the checker my coupons, I leaned close to the register. I should have realized the move was a mistake. The checker began to scan the item and the electronic register broke. Refused to operate.

The malfunctions are not from my cold or hot hands because the same result occurs with my use of a stylus on computer touch screens. Joseph is aware of this anomaly and warns me to stand back from his computer. "Stay back at least four feet. I don't want any disruptions to my pc."

I am fairly adept at using various computer programs. I have produced power point presentations, inputted formulas and charts into Excel, wrote basic HTML for newspaper ads. However, when something goes wrong, I panic.... "Joseph! My computer is not responding" or it stuttered or it blacked out or any of the many things that can trip up a user. The computer senses my antagonism towards it and no matter what fixes I may try; they will not work. I now know what to do when it freezes. I shut the machine down. Once I attempted a hard drive shut down by pushing the on/off button. No response.

I held it down for a few seconds, tried again and again. No response. After 10 or 15 minutes the computer was still on and truly frozen. "Joseph!" Needless to say, Joseph appeared, pushed the on/off button and the computer complied.

At times, Joseph can fix computers by being next to them. He was known for quickly reviving computers out of sluggishness, virus attacks, hardware failures or user error. Employees would specifically ask for him over other administrators.

The following story was told to me by several workers: One day a user stated that her computer was malfunctioning and certain programs weren't working. Joseph sat down in front of the machine, quickly scanned some data, humphed, and then stood up. "I can fix this. You are lucky I brought just the right tool and I will have your computer up and running in no time."

"Oh really? Thank you so much!"

Joseph pulled out a necklace hung with shark's teeth, beads and shells. He mumbo jumboed an incantation while shaking the necklace above the computer screen.

The computer seemed to be showing signs of life.

"Shall I save your file?"

"Oh, yes, please."

"Okay! Try it now."

The user sat down, hit a few keystrokes and all was well. His techniques have been well remembered and were proven on another occasion. He relayed this incident to me.

Joseph was called to check on a user's malfunctioning machine.

"What can I do for you?"

Madeline looked up, "Nothing. Just stand there."

She typed a few strokes on the keyboard. "Uhg! I don't believe it. Okay, you can leave now."

Joseph was perplexed, "What happened?"

"Never mind!"

Returning to his office, another co-worker explained "She heard that you can fix machines by standing close by. She wanted to prove this legend was wrong."

* * *

My habit of bending and crunching key cards and disrupting electromagnetic pulses applies to non-magnetic and non-electrical items and situations as well.

I was one of 200 citizens called for jury selection. In the waiting room everyone was given an eight-and-a-half by eleven-inch laminated paper written with their juror number. With little to do other than reading or working a jigsaw puzzle, I made a point of looking at most everyone else's card. Everyone held an uncrumpled flat card. My card was the only one that was already prefolded into quarters. What were the chances? I chuckled as I reminded myself that a prefolded paper need not be crumpled nor folded any further by my twitchy sweaty hands. At least it was paper and not an electronic device.

It is odd the little things we keep in our minds. This propensity to be aware of eccentric habits was still evident during the selection of 12 jurors and the subsequent trial. We were instructed to leave our notebooks on our seats. Eleven jurors placed their notebooks right side up with the number easily being read as one faced the chair. Again, I was the only one to place my notebook down at a 90-degree angle. This was a consistent unconscious idiosyncrasy for the 10 days we served on jury duty.

Sitting on a 10-day trial tested my analytical skills, recall ability and attention to detail. I realized that if I want to do something, anything, I had better learn as much as there is to know about the subject and pay attention to detail.

Now I consciously try to note what I am doing with my hands as well as my fingers. It serves me well on key strokes. I should plan to take a course on repairing and building electronic hardware. The knowledge might improve my relationship with electronic devices. That is if my electromagnetism doesn't interfere with the equipment.

On Cleaning House *

As you know, I am a one-push-button type of gal. Aside from not being enthused about shopping for food; laundry is the foremost disliked home maintenance task. Why isn't there a program that will send my laundry to 'The Cloud'?

The single "Most Wanted" list is for missing socks. The number of socks missing (or in 'The Cloud') has grown to 30. Luckily, due to an extensive assortment of hand-me-down clothing and linens, (A-hem, hoarding) I do have enough clothing to last a month of turnover; therefore, the number of times and amount of time spent washing is tolerable at one day per month, and never to be done on New Year's Day. Belief in the superstition that what you do on the first day of the year will follow for the rest of the year, saves me from unpleasant chores throughout the year.

Clothing is sorted only if everything does not fit the size of the washer's holding capacity. Thus, my whites have taken on a pink tone and a few shirts have a tie-dyed look. The color pink is not desirable for the man in my life. He prefers tighty-whities. The result is a real benefit for me, as he has taken on the task of handling his own clothing.

In 2006, a company created a perfume exuding an "earthy and fruity aroma" called Eau de Stilton. My viewpoint is-why buy perfume, when the same result can be had in a washing machine? With frugality in motion, I reduced the number of paper towels used in food preparation and clean-up, and increased the use of linen kitchen towels ensuring a good amount of food staining on each towel. And as my habit is to not sort, these towels are added to one load along with jeans and shirts. If any lingering food odors make my man hungry, I hope it is for me.

As a younger inexperienced homemaker, I tried to show off my skills to a potential future husband. John was an engineer on a fishing boat and was hardly domesticated. Some men do need to be reminded to change their clothing at least once per week. He may have thought that the musky odor of testosterone build up would enhance his attractiveness to a mate.

Some men also need to be reminded to keep up on house cleaning chores. He had left a washed load in the washer for a couple of days. I considered that I could be helpful by sorting his laundry which would demonstrate that I had some competency in housekeeping. I supposed a hot dryer would get any musty odors out, and if it didn't, oh well, John, being accustomed to diesel and fishy odors, wouldn't notice. Into the dryer, I threw the whole load. About 10 minutes later, John heard the dryer running.

"What are you doing? Did you rerun the clothes through a wash cycle?"

"No. What for? They are already washed."

Exasperated and shaking his head, he replied, "Those clothes need to be put through the washer again. They are going to smell musty!"

Hmmm. Sounded like he had that experience before. He immediately pulled the clothing out and shoved them into the washer for a second wash.

That must have been the deciding point for him, as he later married someone else. After that, rarely did I show any 'wifely' or housekeeping skills again.

For the past 35 years, I have tossed kitchen towels in with shirts and pants. So what if my clothing smells a bit like food. Isn't food the way to a man's heart? I read that in a cookbook entitled "The Settlement Cook Book–The way to a man's heart". I have the 24th Edition, published by The Settlement Cook Book Co. and printed by The Cramer-Krasselt Co., in Milwaukee, Wisconsin in 1941. The book states the recipes are from The Milwaukee Public School Kitchens Girls Trades and Technical High School Authoritative Dietitians and Experienced Housewives. What is so interesting about the recipes from that era is that many do not give a temperature reading other than 'place into a hot oven'. I love that. Or generalizations like 'if the gravy is not thick, add a bit more flour.'

My great-grandmother was a baker and I did inherit some baking skills from her. "Quality ingredients in a carefree chaotic kitchen" is my mantra. Through chaos comes creativity. You will often find me with a glass of wine in one hand and a wooden spoon or sharp knife in the other hand tapping to music. That formula is when the finished dish turns out the tastiest.

Reading recipes while I cook is too time-consuming and confusing for me. Jumping back and forth to the ingredient list for the next step to follow makes it easy to miss something. It is easier to read one step at a time with the measurement in the directions. My inclination is to dissect similar recipes, then synthesize the ingredients into my own version in my head and make adjustments to my taste.

Joseph, the scientist who follows protocol carefully, now chides me. "Follow the recipe the first time. You can always adjust ingredients later."

"I already know what works, what doesn't, and what ingredients I do not like in this recipe. It will be made the way I like it by adding more chocolate and reducing the flour."

"When the recipes get rough, the chef ad-libs. Just be sure to add enough sugar for me!"

"Don't worry. If it doesn't taste good, there is always the grocery store."

Desperate for some chocolate cake, but not interested in the overly sweet commercial cakes with chemicals and preservatives, I reviewed two popular cake recipes, and then synthesized the ingredients to my taste. The result was much more successful than following the individual commercial recipes I had baked in the past.

Here I will share with you my synthesized recipe.

Heather's Chocolate Cake

Cake Instructions:
- Prepare a Bundt pan or cake pan by greasing and then dusting with flour extremely well. I use butter.
- Preheat oven to 350 degrees.
- Boil 1/2 cup water and 1/2 cup regular brewed coffee; add a rounded 3/4 cup of cocoa powder to the hot liquid, stir until it is smooth and pasty. Add 1/2 cup olive oil, stir, and then add a scant 2 cups of sugar. Beat these ingredients until well combined.

- In a separate bowl sift together a scant 2 cups flour (1 & 7/8 cups), 1 1/2 teaspoon baking powder, 1 1/2 teaspoon baking soda, 3/4 teaspoon salt.
- Next, add your flour, baking powder, baking soda and salt to the cocoa mixture. Beat until slightly incorporated.
- Add pre-mixed 2 large eggs, 1/4 cup plain yogurt, 3/4 cup milk, 1-teaspoon vanilla extract, and 1-teaspoon orange liquor. Beat until a smooth batter forms.
- Pour mixture into your prepared pan and bake for 55 to 60 minutes in a Bundt pan until a skewer comes out clean when tested or bake for 30 to 35 minutes if using layer cake pans.
- Remove cake from oven and let cool for 5 minutes.
- Remove cake from pan and let it cool completely on a rack before icing.

Notes: I always beat by hand with a wooden spoon. Once I tried mixing a cake with an electric mixer. The result was too homogenized and dense for our taste. We are partial to cakes and breads with a more rustic and airier texture.

The ingredients can be adjusted to your liking. More or less sugar and cocoa. If you substitute honey, then there should be an increase in the dry measurements and a decrease in perhaps the oil or milk.

Top it with Chocolate Ganache

- Place one pound of semi-sweet chopped chocolate – 70% or less, into a bowl.
- In a small saucepan pour one cup of heavy cream and three-quarter cup of sugar (or less sugar, depending upon your taste and the percentage of chocolate) Stir over medium heat until the sugar is melted.
- Pour the hot cream mixture over the chocolate and stir until it is smooth and melted.

Joseph's review: "This is the best chocolate cake that I have ever had."

I had to concur. I hope you like it too.

Vintage and in Vogue *

(Previously known as "Old Age")

*As we descend into oldness, the things that upset
you as a young person are now unimportant.
BUT – You can still call me Cupcake. –*

They say that those who live to "Old Age" are tough, determined, goal-oriented, and crotchety, AND, I might add, argumentative and bold. Like my mother. She was not afraid of advising everyone on what they had done wrong with their lives.

These are traits that I did not inherit from my mother who attained the impressive age of 97 and still wore flashy clothing.

I am not like that. Live and let live is how I act towards others. I am easygoing. Others say otherwise but that is how I see myself. What will that mean for my future in the coming years? There is a bit of doggedness in me since I had closely monitored my mother and her caregivers in assisted living and nursing homes during her last chaotic years.

Growing up, I was happy and protected without a care in the world. Mother ruled the nest and father had his outside interests of three jobs and occasionally other soft flesh to cuddle. That chapter is in the R-rated version of my story.

As I have mentioned, I believe that I am easygoing. My mother on the other hand was tough and stern. She believed that once you're gone, you are gone. Caput. And certainly, men are caput by the age of 60.

Luckily, her second husband was four years younger than she was. So after 60 years of age, she still had a few more years of X-rated active engagement with her much-loved husband, longer than most women who marry much older men. Or, perhaps to compensate, do the women have other hard flesh to cuddle?

Anyway, I have strayed a bit in this story.

Yes, I have monitored my mother's life through her stays at an assisted living unit, an adult family home, many hospital stays, and a "skilled" nursing facility. The experience was a young person's guide to oldness. What can I say? Yes, those "Old Age" traits should have steeped into my system.

This is what has happened after hitting the 'Old Age' range.

The Physical Aspect:

The eyes crack a slit open to tell it is still dark in the room, and hearing is still a bit fuzzy. What time is it? Eyes open a bit more; the clock usually reads around 6:15 a.m.

When I was working, the morning routine was simple. A few seconds of a whole-body vibrating stretch, throw back the covers, jump out of bed, stretch for two seconds, wash face – "Do I look decent?" I rose and shone. Within five minutes, the act of dressing for success was complete. Hurry downstairs, pour coffee – how convenient to have a coffee maker that can be set the night before and timed to start in the morning. Grab a muffin or leftover breakfast and out the door with a coffee mug in hand. Wow, I was fast, all within a half hour. Why waste time?

After returning home, in the evening, I took a quick shower to cleanse off the grime from the work day and flopped into bed for six to seven hours of heavy sleep.

By the time I reached my fifth decade, the morning routine stretched out and became 45 minutes. A tad slower in all systems and operations.

Sometime in the sixth decade, preparations extended out to an hour. Slowly stretching the limbs was required to move more smoothly. I rose, but the shining did not occur until I arrived at work.

Then retirement came along. There would be a lot of time to do as I pleased. No more hour and a half wasted each day, sitting in my car for the daily commute. What would I do with that time?

After five years of retirement, I have found the following occurs each morning: The eyes crack open a slit to see darkness in the room; my hearing is still a bit fuzzy. What's the time? 2 a.m.? Then 4 a.m.? The usual two-hour phase of restless sleep. My eyes open a bit more, and the clock reads 6:15 a.m. Whatever. Shall I sleep more or get up? If I think about my 'To Do' list, depending upon the urgency of the tasks, my thoughts may drift back to: 'I'll rest just a bit more.' The bed engulfs me and I surrender to the soft feathers which seem to stroke and caress me.

The eyes crack a slit open again. There is a bit of light peeking out from the edge of the curtains into the room, hearing is still a bit fuzzy. What time is it? 8:15 a.m.! Oh! Another two-hour stint.

At this point, I should hurry and jump out of bed. But no. Wait, lying on my right side, that side still wants to stay in bed keeping me warm and comfortable. The left side is ready to move a bit. Wriggle the toes. Yes, fine, they work. Tighten some leg muscles, okay they work. Lift the arms from under the covers and stretch the fingers and hands, and rub the forearms to get some blood moving. The bedroom is cold. Put the arms back under the covers.

Angle my body so my legs hang over the bedside. Can't get up yet, have to stretch the hips and thighs for a moment—oh not too much, the hipbone might unalign itself. Now, ready to sit up and stretch my torso from side to side. Systems are working. 8:30 a.m. Deep breath and some slow, unsteady steps to the bathroom.

Previously, in my working years, I would have been productive at work by this hour. Gone are the good long, full-body stretches that vibrated my muscles enabling me to jump out of bed. What happened to life in the *fast* lane? At this point in my life, I may be in the slow lane–oh well, any lane is good, as long as one is progressing moving forward, in the running so to speak. A lane is an orientation.

The Mental Aspect:

Now, the only thing racing in the morning is my mind. Thoughts about: How my body is working. Am I still able to move without too many aches? What topic will I write about today and what words will I use? The stories swarm through my mind while I am stretching-too exhausted before rising to get the stories fleshed out. Too bleary-eyed to write words down and I must be quiet lest my partner hear my voice–so no tape recorder. By the time I am fully awake, get to the bathroom duties, and partially dress, these many stories of well-thought-out verse are mostly gone out of my head. The threads are gone. It is difficult to retrieve them. So I still ask, "What do I want to be or do? Am I there yet?" Those questions brought me to writing creative flash fiction. A short story can be remembered.

The time previously spent on a morning commute, driving to work, has turned into a commute from the bedroom to the kitchen while counting down the "To Do" lists in my head. There is so much going on; I have too many things on my plate. Wait. I can't even find the plate. Where is the plate? My dehoarding project failed to reduce the "To Do" lists.

There is one substitution for the long vibrating muscle stretch. The movement is found in the meditative exercise of Qigong. To get into the exercising mood I don brightly patterned stretch leggings under a flowing silky pull over.

Morning Qigong exercises are done in the family room. Joseph comes in while I am warming up my muscles by slightly bending and straightening my knees at an increasingly fast clip.

"Are you okay? What are you doing?" he asks, as I am standing, raising myself up and down by bending my knees a little.

"This wakens my body and vibrates my muscles while grounding me to earth. This is a Qigong movement I learned from the hospice classes."

"Oh, does it work? I thought you might be having a fit," he grins.

Squirrel! I spin my head around. Catching a glimpse of movement outside inevitably distracts me from my task at hand. Between distractions and slow movements, I accomplish very little.

9:30 a.m. and the day really begins, as we are ready for a leisurely breakfast.

State of Mind:

By the time we get our act together, it may be too late. My philosophy is that life should start as an old person and work backwards. We would then have more personal wisdom to guide us when we are young. Our own experienced learned wisdom, so we do listen to ourselves. We would have more empathy for others as well.

Some things improve with age. For example, selective memories. We tend to recall the "old days". We may not remember some movies we have seen in the past, but not remembering gives us a wider selection of movies to be seen.

After watching a 2010 remake of *"Dark Shadows"* I commented to Joseph, "I was delighted to hear the dialogue without the overriding music that doesn't match the scene in today's movies."

"You know, we have seen that movie before. Five minutes into watching this, you didn't say your usual comment 'We've seen this one before'."

Astounded, I replied, "Because I really didn't remember it at all!" I find this partition memory loss is acceptable, as Joseph and I would rather watch the more classical movies. The violent scenes and ear-piercing noise in modern movies hold little interest.

Recent memories become more important to us as we remember other people's birthdays and family becomes more important. Persistence in supporting and keeping a family together is valuable. When we were young, we tended to push family away as we "sowed our own oats", and made our independent ways of life. In older age, we return to what is important. Health, family, and true friends.

What is my plan for the future seventies? My plan is to make my own schedule and finally slow down. Enjoy the paradise I built for myself. Enjoy nature and friends. Sit back, relax, write, and discover a new me, one day at a time.

Acknowledgments

Writing these stories has been an enlightening experience. I would not have had the perseverance to complete my stories had I not experienced the hardships of changes in my life.

The brainstorming support system, from my writing groups, has been instrumental in helping me push forward. I thank you all for sharing your time and suggestions with me.

My husband, Joseph, for his total support and sacrifice in missing me during long stretches of solitary writing. I thank you dear for your patience.

John Verdecias and his band Poppa John "Bug" & the Jam Band for generously turning his brother's "Letter to a Friend" prose into a performable song. John and I agreed that Robert's legacy in prose would be a wonderful way to remember him.

I thank all of my friends for simply being there. They provided the basis of ideas and stories.

But, this is not the end of the story; because life, as we know and hope for, is infinite.

Where do we go from here?

About The Author

A story began when various friends suggested that Heather write about her father's clandestine playboy lifestyle. Well, Heather did not know much about her absent father's lifestyle, but she knew her own.

A local county library sponsored a seminar on "Writing Your Memoir" in July 2018. That was the beginning, the inspiration and push needed to gain momentum on writing her life stories.

Her first published life stories appeared in an anthology with four other writers from a memoir group. "Tales From a Writers' Circle" was released in 2023. Then her own story was released in August 2023 "Why Be Idle When You Can Run With Knives", which included color photographs.

Over many years she contributed articles on gardening and attracting wildlife to your yard for a local garden trade magazine and was a newsletter editor for a plant society. She enjoys leading garden tours and giving presentations on gardening.

Heather is working on her third life storybook centered around gardens. She has also transitioned into writing Flash Fiction. Many of her short stories have been published by various publishers. Her Halloween story, *"The Haunt",* can be found on Spill Words. Contributions to an anthology: *"The*

50-Word Stories of 2023: Microfiction for Lovers of Quick Reads 2023 Elaina Battista-Parsons. The 2024 edition is expected out in November with more of her flash fiction. Her 100 word story "Crushed" was published in "100 X 100 Vol 2" Manawaker Studio May 2024.

Her loves have been centered on travel, trees, real estate, and sports. She lives with her husband and whatever wildlife happens to move in.

www.Heatherhawk.net

Endnotes

1 Chapter 4 – An Unexpected Detour - Medical Error Statistics [2020]: Deaths/Year & Malpractice Rates (mymedicalscore.com)-
Over an eight-year study, more than 250,000 deaths per year are due to medical error in the U.S. The BMJ CDC & Johns Hopkins University School of Medicine

2 Chapter 5 - Dashed Ocean Dreams   http://transpachistory. com/Transpac_History/History.html

3 Ancient Mariners Race   http:/www.amss.us/about-us.html

4 Chapter 10 - The Silver Years – City Girl Moves to the Desert 'California Exodus': "Why are so Many People Leaving The Golden State?   www.wbur.org

LA's population dropped by 176,000 in 1st full year of..... https://abc7.com

5 Moisture appears as shafts or vertical lines through the clouds. https://earthsky.org

6 High winds knock down McDonalds sign onto car in western Arizona story found in www.fox10phoenix.com Other stories can be found on www.kdminer.com

7 (2022, February 21) www.fox10phoenix.com Video captured a dust devil.

8 "Proper Car Washing Guidelines" City of Mesa Environmental Hotline

9 Update in 2024: There were fewer signs as California suffered flooding from excessive rains. The existing orchards were green and we noted at least two newly planted orchards.

10 "The Magic of Water" Water Association of Kern County

Route 66
11 The camels of arizona | never quite lost

12 https://cornerstone-environmental.com/publications/item/goldroad-and-the-oatman-mining-district

www.ingramcontent.com/pod-product-compliance
Lightning Source LLC
Chambersburg PA
CBHW051304120626
46547CB00015B/2083